When Life Stops

Trauma, Bonding and Family Constellation

by Svagito Liebermeister

Dedicated to Meera

Copyright © Svagito Liebermeister 2022
All rights reserved. No part of this publication may be reproduced, stored in a retrieval system or transmitted in any form or by any means, electronic, mechanical, audio, visual or otherwise, without prior written permission of the copyright owner. Nor can it be circulated in any form of binding or cover other than that in which it is published and without similar conditions including this condition being imposed on the subsequent purchaser.

ISBN 978-1-9163644-8-6

Cover painting by Meera Hashimoto

Cover design by Hamido Kardell

PERFECT PUBLISHERS LTD
23 Maitland Avenue
Cambridge
CB4 1TA
England
www.perfectpublishers.co.uk

Acknowledgements

This book is an outcome of the trauma healing process I went through after the sudden loss of my beloved wife and life partner, Meera. Without feeling her continuing love towards me this would not have been possible. She taught me that love is beyond body and mind, beyond time and space. Her aliveness, joy and innocent heart live on inside my heart.

In leaving a huge legacy of paintings and her art therapy work, she helped to shift the focus of my work more towards creativity and towards the unknown, or better the 'unknowable'. I am now doing things I could never have dreamt I would ever do in my life.

Osho and Meera continue to be my greatest sources of inspiration.

I am also very grateful to Anu, and her amazingly loving support, including her very valuable feedback on each chapter of this book, to Pankaja, who helped me with the editing in a very sensitive way, and to Hamido for doing another really beautiful design.

I also feel deep gratitude to so many friends, who were there for me in the most difficult period of my life, to the whole Meera Art Academy team and their dedication to continue Meera's work, to Ingrid and her loving, down to earth way of session giving, to many of my teachers, including Bert Hellinger and Peter Levine, whose discoveries are one of the foundations of this book. I also want to mention all my organisers in many countries, who continue to support my work over so many years and my students, who so courageously open their hearts and wounds in trust and allow me to accompany them on their healing journey.

Contents

Acknowledgements		iii
Prologue		vii
When My Life Stopped (A personal trauma story)		xi
Introduction		xxxvii
Part I: Understanding Trauma		1
Chapter 1	What is Trauma?	3
Chapter 2	Dissociation	21
Chapter 3	Shame and Guilt	43
Chapter 4	Bonding and Collective Trauma	67
Chapter 5	Systemic Constellations	91
Part II: Healing Trauma		115
Chapter 6	A Somatic Approach to Healing Trauma	121
Chapter 7	The Systemic Approach to Healing Trauma	153
Chapter 8	A Somatic Family Constellation Approach	177
Chapter 9	Love and Relationship	193
Chapter 10	The Role of Meditation	211
Chapter 11	Creativity as a Healing Factor	225
Part III: Working with People		241
Chapter 12	Principles of Working with People	243

Chapter 13	The Trauma of the Helper	255
Epilogue		271
Appendix		277
Bibliography		279
About the Author		281

Prologue

A Personal Note

From my teenage years, I developed an interest in learning to work with people, driven partly by my own longing to know more about myself and to have deep, loving connections with others, which I missed in those years. I studied psychology and was part of an avantgarde group of students and teachers, but this still did not quench my thirst to experience love and joyfulness, because all the alternative approaches were also still intellectual.

My life started to change drastically when I met my spiritual master Osho[1] in 1980 and entered a meditative path that took me beyond intellectual concepts. I dropped what I had learned at university, participated in all kinds of personal growth groups and now experienced many therapeutic and spiritual approaches through self-exploration. Rather than entering a career as a psychologist as many of my friends did, I joined one of Osho's spiritual communities where I lived and worked for many years doing all kinds of jobs. This completely changed my perspective on myself and on how to be with people. It was only after this gap that I came back to working with people psychologically and

---

[1] Osho is an enlightened mystic, who in his teachings integrated Eastern methods of meditation with Western therapy techniques. During his life he was known for being provocative to the status quo in his interest to awaken people to their true nature. After he left his body in 1990 his message and meditation techniques continue to spread through his thousands of books, videos and therapy courses that are taught around the world.

now it was quite different from how I had been taught at university. I started to work with clients again, individually and in groups, but now saw them more as fellow travellers.

Since 1986, I have been doing courses and trainings in approximately 25 countries around the world and my clients, to varying degrees, mostly have some kind of interest in personal development, meditation or spiritual growth.

I wrote my first book on Family Constellation in 2006, followed by two more books on therapy and meditation and in 2016 prepared to write another book on trauma, with the idea of bringing a systemic understanding of trauma together with a somatic approach. After having prepared the outline for the book and having done some recordings in January 2017, I went on a holiday trip to South Africa with my beloved wife Meera, who had been my life partner for 25 years. And there the biggest trauma of my life happened and changed me forever.

In February 2017, Meera was taken from me in a dramatic and sudden way while we were both scuba diving together. My life and mind completely stopped and nothing was ever going to be the same again. I went into a state of shock and for weeks and months afterwards was confronted with agony and the feeling that someone had switched off a light and that half of me had suddenly disappeared and died as well.

I lost all interest in my own work and the only thing that kept me going was the urge to take care of Meera's paintings and her work with people. She had been a well-known painter and art therapist for almost all her life. It became my mission to present her work to the public, preserve her art for future generations and support her team of assistants to continue the trainings and creativity courses. I created the Meera Art Foundation (MAF), organised many exhibitions around the world and was part of the trainings that Meera had developed over many years. With much help from many sources we even created a small permanent museum in Italy, the Meera Art Museum (MAM), where some of Meera's paintings are displayed

Even though I picked up my own work and courses as well, my whole attitude and interest started to take a new turn. Personally and professionally I became more focused on meditation, on what I consider important in life and on exploring what the essence of authentic creativity is.

Now 5 years have passed since my world fell apart and I felt it was time to complete this book project. It happened in a different style than originally anticipated and I have included my own experience of losing my beloved wife. In this way, what I have learned about trauma, my experience in working with systemic constellations and body-oriented trauma therapy over many years and my own direct experience of trauma are interwoven throughout the book. This may help to bring theoretical understanding together with a direct experience.

To allow the reader to clearly distinguish between teaching, personal experience and case studies, I have written all personal experiences, all case studies and also all practical exercises and meditations in italics within the main text. So, the reader can choose to leave out or include those parts while reading the book. I also decided to include a chronology of the course of events that led to Meera's passing, which is very personal and may not exactly fit into a teaching book. I decided to include this personal story in this book, because this may touch the reader on another level that is not intellectual. After all, learning to work with trauma needs the ability to resonate with another person. The reader is, of course, free to skip the following chapter and just move onto Chapter One.

From my perspective, all healing – including trauma healing – is only possible through love and compassion, and by developing a witnessing capacity that helps us to be more aware of ourselves and not remain identified and completely taken over by the trauma responses that happen within the body and mind. In my own most painful moments, I often received a message telling me to just be there with what is happening, allowing myself to feel it without escaping it. At the same time, there always came the moment where I felt that for now it was time to let go, not to indulge in pain and move on to doing something else.

When My Life Stopped

Chronology of events that led to my personal trauma

If you decide to read my personal story, then I suggest that you pause sometimes and observe your own emotional or physiological responses and how your body is dealing with them. It may trigger some personal trauma memory. Later in the book you will find suggestions on how to process trauma memories.

I was on a holiday in South Africa with my wife, Meera, after a longer period of work. I have to explain that my wife is an artist and art therapist and gives courses all around the world, while I also work as a therapist course leader in many countries. My wife, Meera, is from Japan, while I am German, but we both primarily live in Germany, with homes in India and Japan too. We both have to plan our schedules carefully to be able to spend enough time together.
 It was one of those nicely planned holiday trips; our first time to South Africa, where we wanted to combine a safari tour with scuba diving in a famous diving area. We usually go scuba diving once a year. We both like adventure holidays and usually I am the one to plan everything, while Meera enjoys coming along and being surprised. So, as usual, I had planned and booked a tour with a rented car; first to the Kruger National Park, then to the coast for a few days of diving before flying back to Europe and then onto Japan to start our work tour that would take us through many countries.

I carefully chose good lodges; I wanted my beloved to be comfortable and get the very best. She told me how much she loved my adventurous spirit and we were both excited about the holiday.

We travelled via Dubai, where I held a short course at a yoga centre and where we were also interviewed by a local TV channel on the topic of 'passion'. Each of us spoke for about 5 minutes. Meera was really passionate in her talk; she loved to be interviewed – only later I noticed that she mentioned death three times and how to die with laughter and excitement. It did not strike me as unusual at the time.

We had a wonderful time in South Africa, driving through the National Park, seeing wildlife and staying at different lodges. Both of us are passionate about being in nature and discovering new places. After one

week we reached the north-eastern coast and for three nights we stayed at an exceptionally beautiful and remote beach resort – one night we even saw baby turtles hatch under the bright moonlight. On our first day, the waves were so high that we could not dive, but we did on the second day. The dive guide took us through the waves in an inflatable boat, which in itself was already an adventure.

We then drove to Sodwana Bay, an equally remote location, but well-known amongst divers for its great dive sites. The resort was not as beautiful as the first but

it was the only one in that area. It had a very large dive base due to its great reputation.

On the first day we did two dives in the morning – we even saw a whale shark. In the afternoon, we had a rest in our small, simple bungalow. Meera treated me with so much love and care and gave me a long massage. It was an afternoon of deep melting into intimacy; it was sweet and gentle.

That evening in the restaurant, Meera asked the waitress if she knew how to dance African style and if she would dance with her if she provided the music. Meera loved dancing and hadn't yet had a chance on this trip to witness any African dancing. The waitress objected by saying that she was a waitress and could not just dance in the restaurant. Meera never gave up easily when she had a good idea; she called the manager and just asked her. The manager agreed and together they planned a dance event for the following night. It was not meant to happen...

When we woke up the next morning after a good sleep, it was a bit chilly and drizzling with rain. I was not enthusiastic about diving in these conditions even though we had already pre-paid everything. I asked Meera if she felt like going out for a dive and she exclaimed – in her usual short and quick way – "Let's go!"

We drove to the beach and met the divers and the dive team. The weather was still unsettled and cold, and it was quite unpleasant to put on the wet diving suit that had not yet dried from the previous day. But surely the water would be warm. I prepared our equipment while Meera went to the bathroom. I left both our cylinders open, as it would be only a short boat ride before we needed to wear the whole equipment.

Still on the beach, the guide explained where the dive site would be, making drawings in the sand to show the reef, while others from the dive crew had already started loading the equipment onto the boat. We all pushed the Zodiac into the water and jumped in. It was packed with about 10 divers plus the dive guide and boatman – quite a lot for such a small boat.

The art of the skipper was to manage to get the Zodiac through the high waves without being hit too hard by them. It was a rough ride and we had to hold onto the rope on the sides of the boat firmly while the vessel was being tossed around by the incoming waves. I kept checking if Meera, who was sitting beside me, was all right and I showed her how to get a good grip on the handle on the side of the boat. She seemed fine and was far from being afraid.

It took about 5-10 minutes to reach the dive site. It is quite a mystery to me how anyone can find a dive site in open sea; there are no signs above water as the reef is sometimes 10 metres or more below the surface, but the guides and the skipper know what to look for and have to trust their experience.

From a Zodiac, being an inflatable boat and therefore flexible and unstable, one has to make a backward roll into the water. You cannot stand up like you would in a bigger boat and jump in legs first. Moreover, as the boat can easily drift, everyone has to go into the water at the same time in order to avoid someone being hit by someone else jumping in later. Hence, the atmosphere on the boat was not as relaxed as it would have been on a larger boat. We felt a bit rushed by the skipper as everyone had to be ready at the same time, and all that just after a pretty rough boat ride. Not much time to gather your thoughts about anything!

Guide and skipper moved around and helped everyone put on their equipment, which was basically the jacket with the tank. Then, before jumping in, we had to put on the fins and mask, and maybe give a last check to see if the regulator worked. Meera and I wore our equipment and I usually helped Meera to make sure that none of her hair was trapped between her face and the mask, which would allow water to enter the mask. While getting ready, I suddenly had the feeling that I should double check both our tanks again, but then I saw the skipper go around and open the valves on everyone's air cylinder. I saw him do this on Meera's, so I relaxed – my biggest and most fatal mistake!

Everyone was now ready to jump, except for a woman who had discovered that her jacket had a rip. Only later I realised that this would not have happened had the dive team checked the equipment properly! So she had to stay on board and could not join in the dive.

It was hectic, with not much time to think. I looked over at Meera to see if she was ready. She was wearing her mask, ready to go. We both did our backward rolls into the water and soon enough were drifting in the water. The dive guide had jumped before us. He was supposed to make sure that everyone was fine before diving down, but he had already dived without looking back. I was afraid to lose him so I gave Meera the okay sign to check if she was also okay and ready to go down. She returned the sign, indicating that she was all right.

I started to dive, headfirst, trying to locate the reef and our group, and looking for the dive guide. Without realising, this created some distance between Meera and me. When I was maybe 7 metres deep, I turned around to see if Meera was behind me. She was not. She had come down in an upright position, and was maybe only 3 metres deep. I looked at her and again gave her the okay sign to check whether she was all right. Something was wrong. With both her hands she indicated that she had some trouble but did not indicate what kind. As I was deeper than she was, I waited for a moment to see if she was able to fix the problem. Sometimes when you dive you get water in your mask, or your ears do not pop open. I was still not alarmed and waited for a moment, watching her.

When she started to go back up towards the surface, I became worried because this meant that she must be having a more serious problem. I started to swim towards her and followed her upwards. I did not suspect that she was in any real danger, which is why I did not rush towards her.

After about 20 seconds – it is difficult to estimate the time in those moments – she came back down. I first thought that she had managed to fix her problem, but as I came closer, I saw to my horror that her head was leaning to one side and that her mouthpiece had popped out of her mouth. I completely panicked and with all my energy rushed towards her, my heart pounding like mad. I reached her in a few seconds, held her body by the jacket and tried to push my spare mouthpiece into her mouth, a quite senseless thing to do when the other is obviously unconscious, but I was in a state of total panic.

While trying to give her oxygen, I didn't realise that we had started sinking fast. She was not breathing and was heavy with all her equipment, so we both had very little buoyancy. When I saw blood coming out of her *nose inside her mask, I freaked out even more. When I finally realised that we were sinking, I filled my jacket with air to bring us up as fast as possible. I embraced her body and together we went up quite quickly, without any safety stop as you are supposed to do in normal conditions.*

As soon as we reached the water surface, I shouted for help. The boat came over. I struggled to take off her jacket with the tank and her weight belt, and with the help of those who were on the boat we pulled her body onto the Zodiac. It was a mighty effort; my mind was blank and my heart was racing.

When I was also back in the boat, we immediately tried to bring Meera back to consciousness. I wanted people to do something for her but everything seemed to be happening so slowly. Someone suggested giving her oxygen and another diver, a Frenchman, who had come with his children, was pressing her heart muscle at intervals to make it beat again.

I turned her body to one side to let any water come out of her lungs, but not much came out. I started to do mouth to mouth resuscitation. She had blood on her face that had come from her nose and my face became covered in blood. I pleaded with her to come back. Her rib cage lifted and sank as I breathed into her lungs. The Frenchman continued pumping her heart muscle, while I talked to her and asked people for help. Not one of the dive team did anything. The skipper tried to get the boat back to the shore through the surf as fast as possible. It bounced heavily through the waves. I screamed, "Not so fast!" while continuing to do mouth to mouth resuscitation. And I kept saying to her, "Please come back! Come back!"

I could not think straight and did not know what had happened. I was desperate.

When the boat arrived at the shore, a tractor pulled it onto the beach and Meera's body was lifted onto the back of a truck. I do not remember how much time it took or how it happened. I kept talking to Meera continuously. I sat next to her on the truck, her head on my lap.

No one else spoke or said anything. I kept talking to Meera. I wanted someone to finally do something. The truck was parked in the parking lot. A woman passed by; she was a doctor. She felt her pulse and said, "She is gone," and, "You can't do anything; it's not your fault."

I was in complete shock and disbelief. It felt as if I was having a nightmare, desperately trying to wake up. I talked to Meera, saying things that I imagined would be good for her. I said, "It is only the body," and "Nothing is happening to you," and "Remember, we are meditators!" I told her how much I loved her. I kept on repeating these words as though in a trance. In this nightmare I kept thinking, "I just need to wake up. But why don't I wake up?"

Everything around me felt surreal. Nothing around me was of any importance, only Meera's body with her head on my lap. I kept kissing her face, eyes and mouth and stroked her body. After a while, I noticed that my body was shivering violently. I walked over to our car, which was parked just next to the truck, pulled off my wet dive suit and put on some dry clothes. I rushed back to Meera's body, which was still lying motionless and peacefully on the back of the truck. All I wanted was to go with her.

Waves of strong guilt passed through me. I had not taken care of my beloved. I was responsible for her death.

Saying goodbye to Meera

I had been sitting with Meera's body on the back of the truck maybe for three hours, maybe longer; I can't remember exactly. I did not know how this accident could have happened. I thought she might have had an embolism or something similar. I still did not want to move away from her body and did not want to see or talk to anybody. The dive crew came and brought some of our belongings and finally the police arrived. Fortunately, the inspector did not ask me any questions.

There was talk of an autopsy. I said I did not want that. I wanted her body to be with me for the night in my hotel room. The police officer phoned the hotel manager and that was sorted. He then phoned his superior who would not allow it. When I insisted, he told me that he could not do anything and that according to the law a dead body belonged to the government. I had no energy left to fight. At least he found a doctor who lived in a nearby town who could do the autopsy the following day rather than in three days' time as the officially authorised doctor would have done.

After a while the hearse arrived to take Meera's body away. They carried her body from the truck, put her in a plastic bag and placed her into the car. I was told they would take her to a hospital some 70 km away, put her in the morgue for the night and then drive her a further 120 km the following day to Richards Bay for the autopsy. I told them that I wanted to come with them.

I followed the hearse in my rented car and asked them to wait at the gate of my hotel where I wanted to collect a few items, like Meera's iPad. I wanted to play some music for her. I wanted her departure to be festive, beautiful and celebrative... not so primitive as it looked like it was going to be. I felt terrible that there was no way to create a beautiful celebration for my beloved's departure from this world. Everything was so rudimentary.

The hearse waited for me, then we drove on. They stopped to fill up with fuel and have coffee... I could not stand it. I wanted to see Meera's body and pleaded with them to drive on, which eventually they did. I followed them for all the 70 km on country roads. While driving, I screamed and screamed and screamed.

After maybe an hour we arrived at the hospital. They unloaded the bag with Meera's body, but before placing it in the refrigerator, I asked them to see her again. They opened the bag, I talked to her, again saying that it is only the body and not to worry. I talked to her, but I talked to myself as well. Certainly, I was the one who was worrying, as the only thing I wanted was for Meera to be well. I played celebration songs from the iPad and placed it next to her head inside the bag before it was put into the refrigerator.

I waited outside in the open and did a dance for her, and kept talking to her continuously. I was there for about two hours. The guard who was sitting outside the morgue took pity on me and asked me if I wanted to see her again. I said 'Yes' immediately. He opened the refrigerator and took out the stretcher. The music on the iPad had stopped playing, maybe because of the cold, so I gave up on that idea of playing music to her.

Finally, my mind started working again. I had to inform many people about what had happened. I was torn between wanting to stay with her and planning all the things that needed to be arranged. Finally, I talked to Meera, telling her that I had to leave and would be back with her the following day.

I felt so very guilty that I had not been able to save her, that I had not been able to keep her body in more beautiful surroundings, that I was unable to stay close to her. I felt so utterly helpless for not being able to create a celebrative surrounding for her. I felt as if the worst thing had happened in the worst place possible. Why had my beloved left her body at such a moment and in such a place?

It took me a whole hour to drive back to our hotel in Sodwana Bay, by which time it was evening. The hotel manager had waited for me and told me that I could use his office for anything I needed to do. I was very grateful because the internet connection for the public was so bad and unstable, although the connection in his office was also poor. Skype did not work as it was too weak. I tried to use my German cellphone but the pre-paid amount was used up after a few calls and to top up my account I needed the internet. It was all so complicated.

I tried to find the phone numbers of Meera's brother and friends in Japan. No one answered. I found the number of a Japanese couple, friends, who spoke almost no English. I told them on the phone that Meera had left her body and asked them to phone her brother, or if they did not have his number, to inform another friend, who could tell her brother. I managed to contact the embassies of Germany and Japan after finding their emergency lines. Luckily, I could use the hotel telephone.

My plan was to take Meera's body back to India and be cremated there, the place she loved and where we could have a proper celebration.

I sent emails around the world and tried to phone India. On Facebook, I put up this post about Meera's leaving:

Beloved Friends,

My most beloved Meera has left her body today, in the morning. I am still in shock and cannot write more right now. Just asking you to meditate with her and give her the send-off she deserves. She was so full of love for everyone – such a gift to have spent 25 years with her. I try to bring her to Pune for her goodbye celebration, if possible.

Fly high, love of my life. Not only me, but thousands will also miss you. But it is only your body that has left and your dances, paintings, laughter and love will remain with us forever.

Even before I had posted this, the news had already spread like wildfire. I was on the computer until late at night – and I still had to pack our two large suitcases. The hotel manager gave me the details of how to reach the town where, the following morning, the autopsy would be performed, and he reserved a room for me in a nearby hotel (but later I discovered that it was 200 km away from it!)

I went back up to our room to pack. I did everything in a trance-like state. My body was shivering with cold, even though it was a warm night. I had to take a hot bath because I was freezing cold. It was so unreal having to pack Meera's suitcase. I was exhausted and after packing I lay down but could not sleep, of course. I dozed off a couple of times, but as soon as my mind remembered where I was and what had just happened, I was wide awake again, my heart racing.

The following day

I had been awake most of the night. I felt as though I was living in a dream, a nightmare, longing to wake up. It was not easy to get out of bed and face reality, but on the other hand I knew I wanted to be with Meera's body again and as soon as possible.

While I was packing the car – it was very early in the morning – a girl from the dive shop came running and hugged me, crying. She gave me one of Meera's possessions and I handed her my still-wet dive suit, saying that she could keep it because I would not be diving anymore. She was the only person I saw from the dive company that day and the only person, so far, who has shared some of my pain and helped me cry. Otherwise I was still in a trance and quite dissociated from everything.

After I had loaded the car, I backed up and hit a bulldozer that was parked just behind me. The bumper was badly damaged, but I could not care less. I checked out from the hotel and started the 200 km drive to Richards Bay, the small town where the autopsy was going to take place. I followed the written instructions given to me by the hotel manager and the journey took me about 2 ½ to 3 hours. Still, it was not easy to find and I was in a great hurry because I wanted to prevent the autopsy from taking place.

I finally found the building and the doctor. Meera's body had already arrived. I wanted to see her and was allowed to do that. Then the doctor started asking questions. I told him everything that had happened and I was very eager to get an explanation from him and reasons why we had not been able not bring Meera back to life. He did not say much, insisting that he had to do the autopsy and that I had no legal rights to prevent it. I finally gave up. He told me that they would cut open her rib cage and stitch her body back together again afterwards. I did not want anyone to touch her body, let alone cut her body open. I tuned inside of myself and received a message to let go and that Meera was fine.

The doctor suggested I should find an undertaker. The embassy had also given me some names, but none were from Richards Bay, so I agreed to use the local undertaker that the doctor had suggested. He arrived within a short time while the autopsy was still underway.

The doctor came out to see me and told me that they could not find a problem with Meera's body. "She was a very healthy lady," he said. The cause of death was drowning, but why she drowned he could not say. All my questions remained unanswered.

Now: paperwork. The undertaker took me to his office first and then his assistant took me to the various government offices where I had to sign papers and give fingerprints. It was torture having to sit and wait in all these offices, while all I wanted to do was to sit with Meera's body. They insisted I had to do this quickly, otherwise it could take a very long time to get her body out of the country.

Meanwhile, the Japanese embassy phoned. Meera's brother had been in contact with them. A very supportive and kind person at the embassy eventually managed to get together all the necessary papers from the Japanese government, and in a relatively short time. I also received many messages by phone, SMS, email and Facebook. It also became clear to me that it would be not possible to take her body to India, so I wondered what the right thing to do would be, and where the cremation should take place.

By early afternoon I returned with the assistant to his office. By now the undertaker had brought Meera's body from the autopsy room and I could finally spend time with her. Her dive suit had been taken off and I washed her body, her hair and face with warm water and soap. I combed her hair and clothed her with a dress that I had brought with me – I had bought the dress for her when we were in Dubai. She liked it very much but had not worn it yet. I also placed a beautiful silk shawl on her that I had bought in China during my last trip. Her face looked so relaxed and peaceful. I asked the undertaker and his assistants to leave me alone so that I could sit with her for some time.

I talked to her and felt her presence very strongly. I got the feeling that she was well, maybe even blissful, but I felt her looking at me as though she were worried. She was concerned about me. I told her not to worry about me, that I would manage and that she should continue on her journey. I told her how much I loved her and wanted her to be well. She was with me all the time. I went in and out of shock and now my tears started flowing uncontrollably. From now on this would happen anytime, anywhere, like a sudden waterfall, with heavy sobbing.

The undertaker returned and wanted to discuss the cremation, which coffin to choose and so on. I reluctantly let them put Meera's body back into the refrigerator. I had received countless messages from around the world. I was informed that neither Meera's body nor her ashes could be brought to India and to organise a cremation as soon as possible. Okay, I thought, not India, but then would she like to be in

Japan? I talked to the man from the Japanese embassy and we decided to take her body to Japan as soon as we could. The undertaker tried to speed things up and pushed me to do all the paperwork quickly, otherwise we would not be able to take her body to Japan before the following week.

My mind was torturing me about what to do and where to have the cremation. It was difficult having to decide all this by myself alone. Was I doing the right thing? I tried to meditate and feel what Meera would prefer. It was Japan.

More paperwork, more phone calls.

I received a message from a friend from Mallorca, who offered to come to South Africa – in fact she had already checked out possible flights. I was very touched and told her that I would come and pick her up at the airport in Durban.

By now it was late afternoon and I needed a rest. That's when I found out that the hotel the manager had booked for me last night was 200 km from where I was; it was actually close to Durban. So I asked the undertaker for the address of a good hotel in town. It was on the outskirts, but I managed to find it after a few wrong turns.

After I had checked in, I spent more time on the internet contacting people, talking to the embassy and to Meera's brother who was very practical and helpful. I talked to friends on Skype and read Facebook comments, which helped me cry.

Then again, I had those strong guilt attacks. My whole life had stopped and nothing made sense. I sat silently, I talked to Meera, I cried, I took a hot bath. I even ate something, because I told myself, "If you do not eat, your body will collapse."

And then I just wanted to sit and sit and sit and disappear in meditation. I had the experience of being out of my personality, as if my mind and body were separate from me. In all my agony it was almost blissful.

The following night I spent awake again, images of the accident always in front of my eyes. I kept a candle burning and wearing Meera's chain with the marble pendant, which I have been wearing since. Even though my energy and nervous system was in a state of high alert, my body had rested somewhat. All I wanted to do was to see Meera's body, spend more time with her and get her some flowers, which I had not been able to do so far.

The following day

Without breakfast, I checked out early and asked for instructions on where to change money. I was told to be careful in that part of town, as it was not a safe area. I also wanted to find a flower shop.

It was again a puzzle to locate the bank in the shopping mall. I parked the car and wandered around without finding it and finally asked in a small shop. The shop keeper was very kind and walked me to the bank and also told me where I could find a flower shop. With some money in my pocket, back in the car, I eventually found the small flower shop and bought all the roses they had and some tealights as well.

The next challenge was to get back to the funeral company. I had memorised the direct way from the hotel, but after having driven around and around so many times it was hard to figure out which way to go, even with my good sense of direction. In this small town everything looked the same.

When I finally managed to get there, with all my roses, I told the staff I wanted to be with Meera undisturbed for some hours. They took her body out of the cooler and prepared a small space in the garage where I could sit with her. I placed all the flowers around her body, lit the tealights and played celebration songs from my iPad. Finally, alone with her and undisturbed... except for the sound of the noisy generator that turned on every few minutes. .

I felt Meera's presence very strongly. She was smiling at me and telling me that she was in a good space and that I should not worry about her. I saw her looking at me with so much love and care. She was concerned about me, but I promised her that I would be okay. I talked with her about so many things and in between, these strong guilt attacks started hitting me. I sometimes danced and sang to her in a shaky voice and sometimes sat silently. I wanted to give her a beautiful send off.

The atmosphere in the room was indescribable; it was as if a huge space had opened up where there was no past or future. There was so much love, silence and sacredness. I had only ever experienced this once before when my master Osho left his body.

Several hours passed in no time. The undertaker returned and reminded me of the many things that still needed to be done. I had to return to the practical world and again and leave Meera's body. Some more paperwork and signatures, and we also had to decide about the coffin. It was already late afternoon and I had to pick up Chetana from the airport. I told the undertaker I would return the following day to sort out everything and to pay him.

Thankfully, the 200 km drive to Durban airport was mostly on the highway. I was driving fast, over the limit, and was stopped by the police. I paid a fine and they let me go. Once in a while I had to stop to adjust the front spoiler, which had also been damaged, probably when I drove too fast over a speed breaker. It was no longer firmly attached and made a loud noise.

This time I had no problem with finding the airport and arrived on time to pick up Chetana, who landed with an evening flight from Mallorca.

We hugged and cried.

It was my first meeting with a friend since Meera left, which felt like an eternity ago, even though only 2 ½ days had passed. I was careful not to tell the whole story too many times; I still needed to function in this world. But I was glad that a friend had come, and that all the local paperwork was now completed. Although it had been decided that Meera's body was going to Japan, so many things needed still to be arranged.

At the airport I changed a large quantity of money, some of which was to pay the undertaker, and then we drove off looking in a small neighbouring town for the hotel that the manager in Sodwana Bay had arranged for me. We found the hotel, but there was no reservation and it was full. I phoned the manager; he told me it was a different hotel, a guest house. Again, it took a long time to find it; it was a very simple place. We were both quite exhausted, Chetana from her long journey and me from the continuous release of adrenaline. When we arrived, there was an urgent message for me from a police investigator who had been trying to get hold of me for two days. I phoned the number and told him he could meet me the following day at the same guest house.

xxx

I opened Facebook, read the many messages and wrote another post:

Thank you for all your hundreds of messages. Each time I read about your love for Meera it helps me to cry. I am so immensely grateful for your love for Meera and for me. I feel like one half of me has departed.

I try to do my best and find out how to deal with everything in the way she would have loved. It seems legally impossible to bring her body back to India, maybe her ashes. After sitting with her I was feeling that she would like to be cremated in Japan. So I am trying this now.

Whenever I am able to, I will answer you all individually, but I am too overwhelmed right now. I want to share with all of you whatever Meera has left on this shore of her incredible energy and love and paintings, so it can enrich everyone's life. I have never met a more generous and giving person with so much love for people. And I can read from your messages that you also felt her totality in everything and her joy and love.

I can't find any other words right now.

I feel that she is in a very good space, full of light and smiles. Please celebrate her leaving with hugs and dances and laughter.

I write again.

And later I posted:
What an explosion of love all around! Thank you, thank you, thank you.
This was Meera's speciality, to bring people together. She was a Master in touching people's hearts.

Now she gave us her last gift, bringing us all together in love. What a way she had!

Now it was time to be alone and silent. I could not sleep much, but at least my body could rest after all this driving around. My heart was in agony and in my mind I only saw pictures of Meera's accident.

The following day

Early in the morning, I left with Chetana and drove the 200 km back to Richards Bay. I was again thinking that it was perhaps not a good idea to delay the cremation for so long by bringing Meera's body all the way to Japan.

When we arrived at the funeral company, I asked the undertaker how long it would take to arrange a cremation in South Africa. He looked at me in bewilderment as if I were crazy. Now that he had organised everything, all the papers and the transport to Japan... I could see that he was proud that he had managed to arrange – he knew some people at the airport – for her body to travel the very next day! And now I was asking this? I told him that it was just a question.

Chetana wanted to see Meera's body – I no longer had the feeling that I needed to see her. I had already said goodbye to her the day before, but nevertheless visited her with Chetana. Something was different this time. I felt Meera was no longer close to her body. It was now only an empty shell. My beloved had left and was spreading her energy into the universe.

I paid the undertaker who told me that all was arranged and that Meera's body would travel with us the next evening on the same flight to Dubai.

It was late afternoon when we finally reached the hotel. The police investigator was already waiting for us. He was very kind and questioned me about what happened before and during the accident. He was upset with the other policemen, who should have informed him immediately and had not properly secured all the evidence. He should have been the one contacted in the event of any dive-related accidents.

Also, he could not say anything about what might have happened to Meera. I showed him her dive computer and her GoPro dive camera. His wife, who had come with him, tried to extract the data from the computer, but was unable to do so for some reason. They took all the items with them and he said he would return again the next morning.

More Facebook posts:

The one thing that eases my pain slightly is to feel the love that everyone has for my beloved Meera and the love she provoked in all of us. It may take me years to get over this loss and I do not know right now if ever I will manage. But now it is this moment. I read all your messages over and over again, so inexpressibly beautiful as if for a moment we all became one.

She always said to me, "Take care of me!" To feel that in her last moment I was an utter failure to do so is very painful. I was with her and still not close enough to save her life. What a blow to my ego and a lesson from existence that we are just a small drop in the ocean and have nothing in our hands. Ultimately it is existence that takes care of us.

I can fill a whole book with stories about her and our almost 25 years of life together and I know you too have many stories to tell. Gladly, I will listen to some of them and maybe collect them if you want to share.

But right now I have to keep reminding myself that it is important to not only feel my loss and what is no more possible, but also to be aware what is good for her and would help her on this unknown journey we are all going to take one day – a reminder to also live the joy, totality, trust, compassion and spontaneous expression she embodied.

I feel her very much around everywhere and keep talking to her and she is always smiling her unique Meera smile – just the way she did when she was in the body.

No words.

Thank you for listening to my personal sharing.

My last day in South Africa

In the morning, Chetana helped me to pack Meera's suitcase properly and put some order into all her things. I threw away almost all the dive items.

As promised, the investigator returned together with his wife. We sat down in the lobby and he said he had to tell me something that he had found out. Although he was not supposed to tell me, he felt he should let me know. My heart immediately started pounding. I called Chetana to come down and hold my hand.

The investigator said that he had found out that Meera's air cylinder was closed. She had no air to breathe. He had checked Meera's camera and the reason why we were unable to read the data the day before was because there was too much data to transfer to the computer. Meera must have taken some photos at the beach and had forgotten to switch off her camera.

The camera was running and recording everything that was going on.

From the recording he could see that, when Meera was under water, there were no air bubbles escaping from her mouthpiece. He concluded that there was no air coming from the tank. Someone must have turned it off by mistake on the boat. Because we went down so fast, Meera had not realised that there was no air coming from the tank. There must still have been a little air in the hose for the first few breaths, but when she realised that something was wrong, she was already three metres under water. For some reason, she did not make it back to the surface in time before passing out.

On hearing this, I almost fainted. I could hardly get up. I struggled up to my room, sent Chetana away, and screamed and beat the cushions. They had killed her! I kept going for some time, while Chetana was becoming increasingly worried about me.

When I eventually came down, the investigator was still there with his wife and their computer, writing reports and examining data. He asked me to leave both of our dive computers with him (Meera's and mine) and also kept the camera chips as evidence. He told me all this would be returned to me after the investigation was completed and that I would be contacted by the police – something that never happened!

It was already past our check-out time; the investigator asked the hotel to let us stay so that he could be with us as long as needed. He was very kind and sensitive.

My mind was going round in circles. What should I have done differently? How could I have saved Meera's life? On and on it went in my head – there were times I wanted to hit my head against a wall.

Finally, we had to leave for Durban to catch our evening flight to Dubai. Chetana would be on the same plane, and then from Dubai she would fly back to Mallorca while I continued to Tokyo.

During the car ride, I asked Chetana if she had ever deliberately crashed a car. She looked at me with big eyes and said, "No!"

I said, "Neither have I," and "How about doing something that we have never done before?"

We never went as far as actually doing this 'something', but on the highway to Durban we had to stop a few times because the front spoiler had started to twist itself around the front axle. We literally just made it to the car rental place where the car stopped dead in front of it. We couldn't have moved a single metre more.

On the way to the terminal building, we saw an African street singer playing on his guitar. This was the first African live music I had heard on our whole trip.

I said to Meera: "This is for you!" I stopped and danced for Meera next to the street musician who was so happy that a foreign tourist would dance to his rhythm.

I was leaving South Africa with the body of my beloved Meera in the hold while I was in the passenger cabin. I lay down as if dead – something of me had really died. The only signs of life were my tears running down my cheeks relentlessly.

Introduction

Trauma has always been a part of human life, but only in approximately the last 30 years have medical and health professionals slowly become more aware of the immense impact that trauma has on human life and developed treatments for traumatised individuals that are more tailored to meet their physiological, mental and emotional conditions.

It is now increasingly recognised how much therapy actually deals with trauma states, which may be the reason why trauma and trauma treatment has become a major topic amongst many health professionals nowadays, as well as in spiritual circles in general. Any therapist who wants to be contemporary in his field has to be, if not trained in trauma therapy, at least 'trauma informed'. It even seems sometimes that most human suffering is related to trauma in one way or another. And it is truly important to create a trauma informed social environment, because in the past trauma was not sufficiently acknowledged, nor appropriately treated. Individuals who suffered from trauma and sought professional help were often treated in a way that made their symptoms or suffering worse, or they were further traumatised by those who were supposed to help them.

In everyday life the word 'trauma' is sometimes used like a buzz word and people call an experience 'traumatic' when in fact it was simply unpleasant or painful. Obviously, not all challenges and problems we face in our lives can be called traumatic and not all issues that clients bring to a therapy session need trauma therapy. Whether an experience is traumatic for a person, or only painful, depends on the event in question and largely on a person's ability to deal with it – something we would also call his personal 'resilience' (we will come back to this later in the book). Genetic dispositions play a role in it, the family history and personal upbringing, as well as one's previous life history and to what degree one has been able to complete past experiences on a physiological, emotional and mental level. In order for an event to be traumatic, it needs to overwhelm a person's capacity to function in an integrated way and respond appropriately. Freeze or dissociation usually indicate the presence of some kind of trauma. Still there are no clear-cut boundaries between what is trauma and what is not, as human experience is too multi-layered.

Trauma can impair personal development and also one's progress on a spiritual path. Therefore, it is important to process a traumatic past, whether this is individual or collective, and reclaim the life energy that has become tied up around a traumatic event and prevents our further development. There is a saying that the trauma you heal will become your strength and the trauma you avoid will ultimately destroy you.

The healing process of trauma can become a catalytic agent for a profound spiritual transformation and what can destroy a person's life can also become his greatest motor for an inner revolution. Whether trauma remains a destructive force or becomes an awakening force depends on many factors, which in their totality we cannot always be conscious of, just as we as helpers never know for sure if we are able to be of help to someone or not. Even though in principle we all have the innate capacity to heal from trauma, just as we all have the potential to awaken to our full potential, whether we will achieve this in life remains an unknown mystery.

This book is a contribution towards creating more awareness about personal and collective trauma and what serves healing. It focuses on understanding bonding trauma and on summarising the approaches of Somatic Experiencing, developed originally by Peter Levine, for dealing with personal trauma, and the approach of systemic Family Constellation, originally developed by Bert Hellinger, for dealing with the collective aspects of trauma. I will explain how each approach looks at what trauma is and in what way they help clients to recover from it. I will further show my own way of bringing these two ways of working together in one session.

Finally, I try to place trauma therapy in the wider context of awakening our potential as human beings. For this reason, many chapters are accompanied by meditations that the reader can practise by himself. Only a meditative consciousness can take one out of the identification with body and mind into a space where no trauma can ever reach.

Part I: Understanding Trauma

Chapter One

What is Trauma?

Trauma is subjective, which means that it depends on the individual whether an event is experienced as traumatic or just stressful. Therefore, it is very difficult to define. Usually for an event to be traumatic it has to be overwhelming and this does not depend only on what happened, but also on the ability of the individual to handle a particular situation. There certainly are events that tend to be traumatic for anyone and there are others that may just be a challenge for one person, but overwhelming for another. Children tend to become traumatised much more easily, as they still lack the emotional and physiological resilience to withstand and process the onset of a challenging event. Early life traumas, like early separation or witnessing violence or war, can scar a person for life.

We all are equipped by nature with an innate ability to rebound from stressful life situations and we have this in common with our brothers from the animal kingdom. Animals in the wild, even though they face life-threatening situations on a daily basis do not seem to be traumatised, while humans may not ever fully recover from one overwhelming event for their whole life. In order to understand why this is so, one needs to know something about the way our physiology works and what happens in moments when our mind perceives our very life to be in danger.

What psychological trauma really is has only been studied and understood quite late in modern psychology. Even though in the aftermath of the first world war, then later when trying to help holocaust survivors and Vietnam veterans, the research about trauma experienced a boost, but the term *Psychotraumatology* was only coined in 1990 and only since the middle of the 90s have trauma research and trainings gone through an immense upsurge.

In trauma we lose connection to ourselves, to others and to our environment. Trauma is alienation. In some way we no longer feel an organic part of this life; we sometimes feel disconnected from our physical form and from those who are close to us. This may not happen all at once, but sometimes over a longer period of time, which is why it is sometimes hard to recognise.

We have all experienced trauma at some point in our lives, and may also have recovered from it either fully or partially. Healing trauma has the potential to give us exceptional strength and a profound understanding of the mysteries of life. It can be one of the doorways to spiritual awakening. On the other hand, if trauma is not dealt with, it can destroy our sense of joy and aliveness either suddenly or in a slow and hidden way, so we may not even become fully aware of what is happening to us.

In this chapter I will first summarise what trauma is according to a somatic view, relying on various sources, especially Somatic Experiencing, a trauma approach originally developed by Peter Levine. I will also include insights from my own experiences in dealing with trauma.

Trauma is in the body

Trauma is a common phenomenon and we are equipped by nature with the ability to recover from traumatic events. In order to understand this, we need to know a few things about how our body deals with challenge or stress.

Our body is designed by nature to respond to its environment through modulating its level of energy. When we experience a challenging moment in life, our body responds with a number of hormonal and physiological changes. For example, heart rate and blood pressure increase, and breathing becomes faster as our body activates our physical energy and prepares to deal with the situation. When the challenge is over, our energy level goes down, any surplus energy is discharged and we 'calm down'. This happens throughout the day and throughout our life in response to environmental stimuli. It is managed by our autonomous nervous system, which regulates all life sustaining functions and, as the name says, it happens involuntarily and without us being able to control it.

This is a very intelligent design by nature because it means anything that is essential for our physical survival is not in our hands and is done by the body without us even having to think about it. If we had to remember to let our heart beat and our blood circulate, we probably would not survive, even for a few minutes.

So, when we are facing a dangerous situation in life, the eyes and/or ears send a signal to a part of the brain that processes that information, called the amygdala. The amygdala interprets the images and sounds and when it perceives danger, whether real or only imagined, it sends a distress signal to the hypothalamus, which is like a control center for the stress response. It communicates with the rest of the body through the autonomous nervous system, which is responsible for involuntary body functions such as breathing, blood pressure, heartbeat, the dilation or constriction of certain blood vessels and small airways in the lungs.

The autonomous nervous system has two branches, the sympathetic and the parasympathetic, which normally function in a reciprocal fashion. The sympathetic branch is like a gas pedal; when activated, it increases heart rate, blood pressure, breathing, tightens muscles and sharpens our senses. These changes increase our stamina and strength, speed up our reaction time and enhance our focus to an external stimulus. They promote what is called the 'fight' and 'flight' response. After the stress signal is over, the parasympathetic branch is activated, which brings the heart rate down again, decreases respiration and increases digestion. It is like a brake, responsible for the body's rest and digestive function. It undoes the activation of the sympathetic branch.

This self-regulative mechanism can be disturbed or move out of rhythm when the organism's activation level goes above a certain degree, or when our ability to respond to an event becomes overwhelmed in some way. Instead of working in a reciprocal fashion, where sympathetic and parasympathetic activation alternate, they both start to be activated at the same time. Like the power system in a house, when the electric current is too strong, the fuse goes out. In the body, this is experienced as going into shock. It is a combination of high sympathetic activation in combination with a high parasympathetic activation. It can be compared with a car where the gas pedal and the brake are both pressed at the same time. It leads to immobility in a state of high arousal.

Animals use this as a last level of defence against

being killed. When they cannot escape the predator, from one moment to the next they go from high arousal to a completely lifeless state. They 'play dead' and in this way maximise their survival chances as the predator may lose interest and they may still get away. It also serves as a sedative against feeling the pain of being devoured alive.

Humans also are equipped by nature with this defence mechanism. When fight or flight seem impossible, our body activates this protection, which is called the 'freeze response'. This freeze is only meant to last for a certain time, after which the body is meant to come out of it, releasing its built-up level of high charge.

For example, one can see how animals sometimes shake their bodies or tremble vigorously after coming out of the freeze they went into after having been caught by a predator. A gazelle, who has been caught by a cheetah and has been motionless and in a death like state, may come out of the freeze once the predator has removed himself, maybe in order to get his young ones to feed on the prey. Coming out of the freeze, the gazelle shakes vigorously for a few seconds before returning to his herd as if nothing had happened.

Here comes the problem for humans, who often are unable to come out of the freeze response they went into in response to a traumatic and overwhelming event. Like animals, humans are equipped with the 'emergency' reaction of going into freeze when their life is at risk, even if only perceived to be so. In such situations, our neo-cortical functions are overridden by the more primitive part of the brain that is in charge of survival responses and reflexes. In other words, in such life and death situations, we behave in a similar way to animals.

However, when the threat is over, neo-cortical functions take control again and the thinking mind is back in charge. This seems to inhibit us from releasing the immense survival energy that has been activated in the body. One may prevent trembling or shaking that the body would like to do, maybe thinking that this is embarrassing: 'How can I shake or cry right now?'. One may be afraid of the strong release that the body is about to do and prevent it. All this sets the stage for developing symptoms of post-traumatic stress.

So, trauma is not just a painful event. It is an event that overwhelms our system's capacity to respond with fight or flight, so we therefore go to the last line of defence, which we call freeze.

It is difficult to decide theoretically if an event is traumatic or only stressful. Not all stressful events are traumatic, but certainly all traumatic events are stressful. What may be just a challenge for one person may be traumatic for another. It depends on many factors, including a person's resilience, his available support, family situation and other factors.

We all have experienced trauma at some point. We may not be fully aware of it and fail to understand how such events still play an inhibiting or restricting role in our lives. Of course, we may have been able to heal some trauma experiences, while others may be deeply buried in our unconscious and may cause seemingly mysterious physical or psychological symptoms.

While there are more obvious causes of trauma, like war, abuse, neglect, witnessing violence or severe injuries or illnesses, there are also less obvious events that can lead to trauma. These can be minor accidents, medical procedures, loss of a loved one, natural disasters, a difficult birth, being left alone in childhood and many others. It may be that a person was not actually in a life-threatening situation, but only the mind, the amygdala, perceived it and interpreted it as such.

Trauma can happen in the form of a single, one-time event (shock trauma) or as a series of events over a longer period of time that, especially when this happens during childhood, can disturb and impair a child's healthy development (developmental trauma).

Shock trauma and developmental trauma

Developmental trauma can either be caused by a single traumatising event or by a series of ongoing experiences of neglect, abuse or mis-attunement. This usually happens at an early age and has a negative, cumulative effect on brain development and can impair the healthy functioning of the whole nervous system. It is often in connection with relational issues with primary care givers (mostly parents) that disturb the healthy bonding between parent and child (bonding trauma). This can set the stage for lifelong physiological and psychological deficits.

The earlier such traumas happen, the more widespread and long-lasting impact they have on the body and mind. In cases of early or severe trauma, a child cannot fight or run from the threat and therefore the only option is to go into a freeze response. This can become chronic and stay in place even after the threat is over. When children get stuck in a freeze or dissociation response, they then have less access to healthy aggression, have a diminished capacity for social engagement and are more vulnerable to experiences of trauma later in life.

I also want to mention here that traumas can happen in the family system or even in larger social systems, like a whole country. This can affect a person indirectly, and can sometimes span a few generations (systemic and trans-generational trauma). We will discuss this in the chapters on Family Constellation.

Shock trauma, on the other hand, is usually related to a one-time devastating incident that leaves a person in fear and frozen in time. This is the result of an overwhelming event that happened out of the blue, like an accident, which one could not prepare for. Many reported tragedies start with: "It was a lovely day ... Everything was calm as usual ... It was a blue sky and perfect weather ..." This points to the unexpectedness of such events, where we are suddenly taken from a relaxed state into a state of overwhelm, where our body and mind have no time to prepare or get ready to deal with the emergency situation that is ahead of us. It is as if you just wake up in the morning after a pleasant dream, still feeling cosy and warm in your bed and are suddenly supposed to do a sprint and run for your life. It is characterised by high arousal in combination with full shut down.

When we later look back at the course of events, investigate what happened, are able to rewind and remember consciously the moment to moment course of events, we sometimes find certain early signs of danger. We may discover that before our life came to a sudden halt, there were some indicators that something was not quite normal, a hunch about what was to come. It happened like that to me.

I was on holiday with my wife Meera in South Africa at a remote dive site. We were looking forward to a dive, not expecting any danger. It was not a routine trip, as we had to take a boat ride through rough surf to reach the dive spot. So, we were a bit nervous and the rushing of the dive crew did not help us to relax. Signs that should have made me more alert, like the fact that another diver's equipment was faulty and she could therefore not join the dive, were ignored by me. And I did not double-check Meera's equipment a second time before starting the dive.

After some seconds of being under water, Meera indicated that she was having some trouble and started to move back to the surface. I was not directly next to her and deeper under water and started slowly to follow her.

From then onwards, everything happened so fast, but it felt like an eternity: I saw her coming back down after just a few seconds, but as I approached her, I saw that she had lost consciousness. With a pounding heartbeat and in a state of panic, I rushed towards her to give her oxygen, which was useless and obviously too late.

I brought her body up to the surface, screaming for help and with some support we lifted her back into the boat, doing resuscitation, but she never regained consciousness. It all happened within 3 minutes and my beloved wife and life partner had left forever. All my pleading for her to please come back was useless.

I was in a state of shock and numb as if the whole world was far away and the voices of people seemed to come to me as if through water. I thought I was having a nightmare and I would just need to wake up and it would all be over.

I talked to my wife on the back of that truck, where her body was lying in my lap, telling her things about death that I felt would be good for her to hear. I kept on repeating those words as if in a trance and still wondering why I did not wake up. It was like being in a surreal film. All I wanted was to be with her body and to go with her.

A doctor passed to check her pulse and said, "She is gone." and, "You can't do anything; it's not your fault." But that is exactly what I felt. Waves of strong guilt passed through me. I had not taken care of my beloved. I was responsible for her death.

After reading this, I want to ask you, the reader, to stop for a moment and notice any feelings or bodily sensations that come to your attention. Witnessing someone else's traumatic experience or even reading about it may trigger certain reactions in you. Can you track what is going on in your body, in your emotions and what thoughts are coming to you? You may want to pause a moment before continuing to read, write it down and process what is going on inside.

Signs and symptoms of trauma

Whether an event was traumatic for a person or only stressful can be judged by how easily one is able to come back to normal functioning and to self-regulation after the event is over; in other words, if there are any physiological or psychological symptoms that stay on after the traumatic event has passed.

Bodily symptoms often carry a message and have a physiological meaning. There are various indications that one has been facing a traumatic and overwhelming event, including symptoms that may appear immediately – for example, dissociation, hyper arousal, constriction, immobility, feelings of helplessness or guilt, or dizziness. Other symptoms may develop over time and can also be less obviously related to the traumatic event, like persistent bodily tensions, numbness, sleeping problems, memory loss, emotional instability, chronic fatigue, immune deficiency and others. In contrast to body symptoms that are not related to trauma and can disappear quickly, trauma symptoms often stay on for a longer period of time.

Our body is equipped with a mechanism to deal with trauma and also to overcome it. The **freeze response** that I described earlier serves as a defence against being overwhelmed by feelings and sensations.

Dissociation is a form of freezing and often the only option if fight or flight is not an option. We all have experienced such states in different moments in our life – for example, when we are either unable to move, to sense our body, to speak, to feel anything or even to think straight. To varying degrees, such states show up in our life and they also disappear again after some time, at least in most cases. In the case of trauma, we may be unable to come out of such states and remain permanently frozen or dissociated. I will discuss this in more detail in the next chapter.

In trauma, often things happen so suddenly and powerfully that the nervous system's activation can be too strong and our organism is flooded with feelings of fear, panic or pain. In order to protect us from this, our body responds by secreting endorphins, which are like our internal opium or tranquilliser. One can often see that people who have experienced a deep shock cannot cry, or do not seem to be afraid or panicked, or seem not to be experiencing any pain.

In my own experience, I also showed clear signs of dissociation. Everything had happened so fast and unexpectedly that I could not prepare for it in any way. From one moment to the next my beloved had gone from me. We could not even say goodbye to each other. For days, I was in a trance like state, numb towards the world around me. I could still function and do all kinds of practical things that were necessary, but in a certain way I was completely absent. I felt as if I were one of the living dead, as if I were no more part of this world. Nothing had any meaning anymore. The life around me, including all the people, felt as if they were far away and distant. I felt as if I was in a dream or under drugs – the obvious effect of the release of internal endorphins – and I was continuously thinking that it would just take another moment and I would wake up from this nightmare. But that never happened.

Looking back now, it seems to me that dissociating helped me to endure something that I could not have endured otherwise. The only thing I really wanted to do was to sit with Meera's body and let the whole world around me end. In fact, I wanted to go with her.

Sometimes one oscillates between dissociation and **hyper arousal** and both experiences stem from the same part of the brain, the limbic system, when it is highly activated.

In my own case, I was so activated that I barely slept for a whole week and whenever I dozed off for moments in the night, I was immediately wide awake and alert, remembering what had happened. I was able to do things that under normal conditions I would be unable to do, or that would even harm my body. Coming up to the surface fast from a dive of 10 metres depth or more was potentially dangerous and could have caused severe injury. My mind was also running wild with repetitious thoughts and worries. I was continuously thinking what I should have done differently and my mind was desperately trying to rewind the whole sequence of events and find a different outcome.

Such hyper arousal is often accompanied by a **constriction** in the body, as the nervous system is trying to focus all our efforts on the threat. This can alter muscle tone, breathing, posture and the functioning of internal organs.

In my case, I literately had to force myself to eat anything in the coming days/weeks, as my digestive system was almost turned off, a typical consequence of sympathetic activation. I just told myself that unless I eat a bit, I would not be able to function at all and sustain my energy to take care of the many things that needed to be looked after. My body was completely numb and shut down. After a short while, I also developed a strong pain in my solar plexus area that created a powerful vomiting sensation that continued for days.

*My **sense of hearing** was affected as well. I sometimes heard the sounds around me as if they came from far away. It often felt as if someone had hit a big church bell or a huge drum and I found myself engulfed in its echoing muffled sound.*

Time distortions are also a typical after effect of trauma.

For me, it felt as if my life had come to a stop and my sense of time was completely changed. Being under water felt like an eternity, when in fact as I found out much later it only lasted 3 minutes altogether. Everything else that happened during that week was stretched out as if it lasted for weeks, while in fact it was just 3 or 4 days. It is quite common that after trauma a part of a person's life experience stops at the moment of the event and the sense of continuity is lost.

While on one side there is the activation of the sympathetic nervous system, there is also the overstimulation of the parasympathetic nervous system. Therefore, on one hand one may feel very charged, but on the other hand there can be feelings of extreme **helplessness, immobility** and a state of freezing.

I can still remember that in the evenings I would sometimes be shivering with cold even though it was a warm climate. My body was so immobile at times that I could just sit and do nothing for hours, watching my mind going in a roller coaster circle. At other times I felt so much activation and emotion that I was hitting cushions in my hotel room...but we will come to this later.

Trauma related **guilt** is another after effect of trauma. It is a feeling or belief that one should have done something differently at the time when the event occurred. In my experience, it was a very torturous feeling as if I were being eaten up from inside. I will discuss more about such feelings and how to overcome them in Chapter Three.

Besides the symptoms described, there are many others that can show up at a later moment after the event. There is no general rule about which symptoms show up when. The following list is taken from Peter Levine's book *Healing Trauma*:

Hyper vigilance, flashbacks, strong sensitivity to sound or light, hyperactivity, nightmares, abrupt mood swings with frequent emotional outbursts, shame and lack of self-worth, sleeping problems, inability to handle stress, avoidance behaviour, attraction to dangerous situations, addiction, panic attacks, amnesia, relating difficulties, fear of death, self-destructive behaviours. Long-term symptoms of trauma can include many psychosomatic illnesses and chronic body pains, chronic fatigue, digestive problems, depression, inability to respond to others or relate in a consistent way or a feeling of detachment and isolation.

Compulsion to repeat

People who have suffered trauma often show a compulsion to repeat their experience in an unconscious attempt to resolve and heal the past trauma and integrate its inherent survival energy. These re-enactments are sometimes played out in repeated accidents, in relationships or work situations. They may also show themselves through bodily symptoms or psychosomatic illnesses. A person, who grew up in a war zone, for example, may find herself working as a relief worker in a country where there is –or has just been – a civil war. A woman who was raped may time and again be attracted to abusive men. Often events or accidents that appear strangely repetitive may have a cause in an unresolved past trauma. It is often not easy or obvious to find such connections, as on one hand there is the unconscious wish to heal, and on another there is the tendency to avoid remembering the past pain.

Some of the symptoms I described here, I went through personally. Some lasted briefly and others lasted for quite a long time, but their intensity simply decreased. Later, I will examine what is helpful in reducing these symptoms and preventing the development of PTSD or long lasting aftereffects. There are, however, experiences in life one may not fully recover from and one has to learn to live with some of the consequences.

Exercise

Write down when you experienced dissociation or any other of the symptoms described above. Do you remember if anything 'triggered' these responses? What helped you deal with and overcome such responses? Do you tend to feel more hyper activation or more dissociation in your life and how does this manifest?

Now remember other moments where you had a sense of well-being and joy. What usually triggers such moments and in what situations do you find it easier to connect to such states? Do you make space for such situations to happen? Or what could you do to make room for them in your daily life?

Stop Meditation

A trauma is often like an event that stops us in our tracks. Our life has been running in a certain routine and we may take it for granted that it will continue in this way. We often feel relaxed in certainty and safety. Trauma is as if existence has struck us like lightning without any consideration for our wishes. It can be a tremendous and vehement force, like the hit of a Zen master. That is why trauma can also awaken us to who we really are. Normally, we are identified with our actions and not in contact with our being. Zen masters often remind us that we do not know who we are in our essence, in our center. We only know our periphery and what can be disturbed is always only our periphery, never the center. Meditation is concerned with finding the inner center.

This meditation is taken from a long tradition of Buddhist lamas and one of the 112 meditation techniques described in the book *Vigyan Bhairav Tantra, Volume I, New Commentaries* by Osho. George Gurdjieff made them known in the West as stop exercises.

Whenever you do something, any daily activity, or whenever you have the impulse to do something, just stop. Hold your body and even your breath for a few moments, become like a stone statue without movement. Just freeze and watch. Do not try to be inactive and do not arrange your posture in any way to be more comfortable. Suddenly order yourself to stop. Do it suddenly when you are not aware, without any preparation.

First try this with ordinary activities. Then try it also with feelings or thoughts. Suddenly stop yourself in the middle and watch where the energy goes. It was going out and now you have stopped, so the only other direction it can take is in. But the impulse must be a real impulse, not a false one. When you feel the impulse, suddenly stop without thinking about it. And then wait and see what happens.

Chapter Two

Dissociation

Dissociation is a reaction against being overwhelmed and is therefore one of the most common consequences of a traumatic experience. Such dissociation is very widespread and we all come across it in many ways in our own lives, especially in our modern world, where being overwhelmed is for many people almost an everyday life experience.

Dissociation usually shows when we are stressed or come from a stressful event and attempt to complete another task without giving ourselves enough time to rest or recover. Dissociation is so common in our lives that we tend not to notice anymore that this is what is happening. We may have come home from a stressful workday, and while trying to read a book may realise that we cannot recall anything about the page we just read. Or we may not be able to remember how we have reached place A from place B. Or in an examination we go blank and do not know how to answer a question, even though we actually know the right answer. Many people are completely out of touch with their feelings or their body and live in their minds most of the time – another form of dissociation.

Such responses may not necessarily be related to a past trauma, but they certainly show how overwhelmed we are in our modern, fast moving and goal-oriented world. Our body is often struggling to keep up with the fast pace of our mind and tries hard to supply us with the energy and available resources to fulfil the task in hand. Dissociation is a way of reducing the sensory input, so our brain can still function without being distracted.

I recall how in my childhood when I was deeply immersed in reading a book, I literally could not hear my mother calling me to come to dinner. Imagine walking around in downtown Tokyo at night with all the traffic, advertisements and sounds. In order to function and find your way, your body may need to dim or blank out certain sensory inputs, so you do not become overwhelmed. When someone asks you later about what you saw or heard, you may be able to report only a tiny fragment of what your senses really perceived. Most of what actually happened and your eyes registered never reached your awareness, but was filtered out by the thalamus, a small brain structure that functions like a gatekeeper who decides what should be allowed to reach to the cerebral cortex.

Everyone may not agree in calling this dissociation as it is a long way from the pathological end of the continuum, but still this is what dissociation actually means. We live in a dissociated world. Without the capacity of your system to dissociate you would find yourself frozen, unable to move or act intelligently many times in your life. Dissociation is like the light dimmer switch in your home, so the room is not filled with a too bright light and your senses are not over stimulated.

Coming back to the city after having stayed for a while in a lonely place in a forest, one may get a taste of how overwhelming this can be. But the people who live in that city all the time may not notice this as their senses are dimmed.

It is a well-known fact that different people who witness the same scene of an accident may all give a different report about what happened. They tend to depict different aspects of the event according to what their system filtered out and that may depend on their own past experiences, their relation to the person involved, their own emotional state at the time and many other factors. Our memory system is not like a photographic plate or a hard disk; it is not recording, but constructing information. It is continuously putting pieces together according to what our brain considers important. Our brain selects what is to be remembered – and emotionally charged events are more likely to be remembered. This is one of the reasons why a traumatic memory becomes consolidated, stable and part of our long-term memory.

Freeze

There is a slight difference between freeze and dissociation. In a state of freeze, one may not be able to move the body, to think or feel anything at all. This state as explained in the first chapter is supposed to last only a short time and animals in the wild usually manage to fully recover from that state through shaking and discharging their aroused energy. Humans often do not fully come back from such a state after a traumatic event, and a part of their energy remains dissociated or split off from their full life energy. In a dissociated state one can still function, but one's full life experience is reduced, 'dimmed'. One may even appear relaxed to others, especially to those who are also dissociated, when in reality a dissociated state is the opposite of relaxation – it is just that the underlying charge is not clearly visible. While a state of freeze is more obvious, a dissociated state is much more subtle and more difficult to recognise, not only in others, but also in ourselves.

Denial

Denial seems to be a form of dissociation, just to a lesser degree. We may deny certain feelings we had about an event, or that the event even occurred, or at least that it was very important. We may deny that we have been affected by an insult, for example, because we may not want to deal with the feelings of rage that surfaced in that moment. So, denial and dissociation function hand in hand. We are dissociated from our feelings and consequently deny the importance of the event that provoked such feelings.

Ways of dissociation

Dissociation can happen with regard to our whole body or parts of our body; it can be related to our feelings, thoughts, behaviour, memory or even related to splitting off parts of our whole personality (dissociative personality disorder). In general, it is a defence mechanism to protect us from overwhelm. Comparing it to the electric system of a house, when there is too much current, either the fuse blows and the whole system shuts down (freeze) or a dimmer reduces the amount of current that runs through the wiring or shuts down certain circuits (dissociation).

People who have out of body experiences or can watch their body as if from above are often dissociated. Victims of rape or people who were attacked by wild animals often report how they did not feel any pain and literally disconnected from their body and could watch their own body from outside.

In moments of strong pain, the body releases endorphins that function like tranquillisers, which is nature's way of protecting us from having to go through unendurable experiences. It may also help us not to become overwhelmed by pain and feelings of panic and fear, so we can still function rationally. This can help the man who is attacked by a wild beast to find an escape route. It can help the woman who is being raped, because not showing emotions will possibly prevent the perpetrator from getting further sexually stimulated. Dissociation can be a life-saving strategy for our body mind system and also a way to escape mentally when physical escape is impossible.

One can also dissociate or feel disconnected from a certain part of one's body. For example, after an accident one may be unable to fully sense a leg or an arm and feel as if this part of the body is absent. I remember a severe childhood accident to my shoulder when I was 5 years of age. My grandmother was holding my bleeding arm while we waited for the ambulance and I kept saying in shock that my arm was gone. I actually did not feel any pain in that moment and later could not remember how I was taken to the hospital in the ambulance.

Memory loss or severe amnesia can also be an aftereffect of trauma. One can either lose the ability to remember certain details of some events or even not remember anything about what happened. Memory loss can occur after accidents, injuries or medical procedures and is a common phenomenon in the case of childhood traumas. By not remembering, or even denying that something like this happened, a child can avoid dealing with overwhelming pain and, if the trauma is directly related to the parents, manage to retain an idealised image of his parents and thus not disturb his relationship to them.

Often, chronic pain happens in a part of the body that is dissociated.

Dissociation can also happen in relation to our feelings or our behaviour. One may not be able to feel pain, fear, anger or have access to any other feelings, or may not be able to express anything at all. People who are in a state of shock can sometimes function and continue with their life as if nothing had happened.

The film *Fearless* by Peter Weir gives an excellent example of what dissociation is. The survivor of an airplane crash, played by Jeff Bridges, is continuing his life without experiencing any fear or pain and remains disconnected from his own family, unable to connect with real feelings towards them. He is in a dazed state and out of his body to such a degree that even his body's allergic reactions seem to have disappeared.

In my own experience, right after Meera's accident, I was quite dissociated from my feeling and at first unable to cry. Only slowly could I allow my tears to come. Especially when I felt the presence of a friend or felt loved could I allow myself to cry. For weeks to come it could happen at any moment that suddenly a wave of tears or sobbing just hit me and consumed me.

In relation to my body, I stayed for quite a while in a dissociated state, sometimes feeling as if I were dead or as if a light had been switched off in my life. When I went to rest at night, my body felt like a corpse, motionless and ready to die. Only after those moments when I could allow deep feelings of pain, agony and waves of crying and sorrow to pour out of me, some part of me came back to life. This happened only gradually and over a period of weeks, but whenever my mind remembered the accident I was easily going back into dissociation.

For many months I had very intense dreams and did not sleep much. When waking up in the morning and becoming aware of Meera's physical absence, I often just wanted to turn over and go back to sleep. It was sometimes an effort to start my day and to get up. Sitting in meditation for one hour helped a lot, as well as giving myself the time and space to function at a slow pace.

As Peter Levine describes in his SIBAM model, a full life experience consists of different elements, called sensation (S), image (I), behaviour (B), affect (A) and meaning (M). When all are present in our experience, then our life experience is full and whole. For example, you may remember how you had a walk with your partner the other day (B), still have in mind the picture of the huge tree you passed (I) and how pleasant the breeze felt on your skin (S) and how you felt fulfilled and happy (A). You understand how important it is for you to take time for such walks (M). After traumatic events, we often become disconnected from one or more of these elements while others are overly associated with one another. You may see a certain type of dog on the street and without knowing why, your body starts sweating. You may not remember in that moment that you were bitten by a dog when you were three years old and you may not be able to distinguish the present situation from the earlier one.

For a while, being at the sea or swimming in the water brought back instantly the memory and the image of Meera's drowning. And with it I could feel the slight activation in my body. While for others swimming in the sea may be associated with joy and relaxation, it triggered fear and pain of loss in me.

A trigger can be a situation, an experience or an event that sparks an emotional or physical reaction, regardless of your present mood. They are very common in people with post-traumatic stress disorder (PTSD). Usually they are tied to our senses as our body remembers something that happened during or before the trauma event and puts us on alert as if the situation is happening right now. Triggers are like buttons that turn on our body's alarm system.

Triggers can lead to so-called trauma related flashbacks, where a traumatic experience is relived partly or fully as if it were happening now. Normally, when we remember an event from the past, it has a certain place in time and history and we are aware that we are remembering something from the past. In a flashback, this timeline is disturbed and we experience a past event as if it is happening now, as if the event of the past is still continuing now. Flashbacks are mostly sensory or auditory in nature and can be triggered by sensory signals.

In some severe cases of trauma, dissociation can affect a person's whole personality and a part of the conscious mind gets split off (dissociative identity disorder). One may not know anymore who one is or may develop different selves.

Understanding dissociation

It is important to realise that by dissociating, our body and mind are trying to cope with an overwhelming level of activation; it is a sign that something is simply too much. So rather than becoming annoyed or judgmental and trying not to be dissociated, which may increase the level of dissociation more, it is better to recognise that this is happening and understand it as a message that our body needs rest or support. Finding resources is a very effective way to help oneself come out of dissociation and overload.

Many times, people do not respond in this way, but feel guilty that they are not present enough and then try harder to be present, or in the body. Rather than respecting the message of the body, this can then create further activation and therefore more dissociation. It is even worse when people think that they are relaxed when in fact they are actually dissociated. Of course, it is not so easy to come out of dissociation alone, especially when dealing with a severe trauma, and one may need to find professional support.

Dissociation often is connected to the freeze response. The difficulty is that the moment we come out of the dissociation or freeze we may become aware of the profound arousal that is underneath, including the feelings of fear or even panic, or sometimes the rage. Noticing this fear or rage may bring us right back into the freeze or dissociation. That is one of the reasons why many people prefer unconsciously to remain in a dissociated state, because then they do not need to face unpleasant and uncomfortable feelings that they would otherwise have to deal with.

One important aspect of trauma therapy is to separate fear from the biological freeze response, to learn to separate feelings from physical sensations. We will come back to this in Chapter Six. We need to develop a capacity to have strong feelings without going into dissociation or freeze and without having the compulsion to get rid of such feelings. Trying to get rid of feelings of fear or anger is also often a fear response; it is fear of the fear or fear of the anger that drives such attempts.

On a physical level, it is about completing the incomplete responses of fight and flight that are held in the body and are stuck in the freeze response. Coming out of freeze, one notices that the body originally wanted to escape or defend itself, but the situation did not allow this or one's capacity to do so was overwhelmed. It is similar to a gazelle that could not escape the cheetah, but that is what the body tried to do. From one moment to the next, it went into freeze, into a seemingly lifeless state. When coming out of that state, the energy of trying to escape is still there and the animal's body will shake vigorously and discharge all this energy before returning to its herd.

When researchers filmed those involuntary movements of animals who returned back from a frozen state and watched those film clips in slow motion, they were surprised to realise that they consisted of the rudimentary running movements that the animal could not complete when trying to escape the predator.

When humans can learn to trust their physical responses and allow such a strong discharge to happen through their physiology, then the need to go back to the freeze is greatly diminished. On a psychological and emotional level, this sometimes means one has to learn to tolerate feelings of anger and fear rather than trying to rid oneself of such emotions.

Meditation

We often feel that rather than suppressing emotions we need to learn to express them. Many traditional therapies are also based on this understanding, which is only partially true. The mystic Osho once explained that expression and suppression are two aspects of the same coin. In both cases we project the feeling onto someone outside. We may suppress the feeling, which is a kind of postponement, as we will have to express it some other time. Or we express the feeling and then the energy has leaked out and we may feel a short relief, but basically, we are depleted.

In this meditation from the book Vigyan Bhairav Tantra (by Osho), one tries to go back to the source from where the energy arises, neither suppressing it nor expressing it.

When a mood or feeling arises in you, do not place it on the other, but find the source from where it arises. If you feel anger or fear or love, do not place it on the other, but remain centered. Remember that you are the source of these feelings and look from where they come inside. Feel the energy of the feeling as it gets hold of your body; allow the movements in the body as if a storm is passing through you.

Then go back to where that energy or feeling arises from inside.

Hints for how to deal with dissociation

It is not always easy to be with feelings of anger, fear or pain without trying to get rid of them or suppress them. When a person is traumatised, they often need help from outside as such feelings can overwhelm the person again, and then the original trauma experience is simply repeated. These feelings are often hiding behind a dissociated state and they may suddenly erupt. This can be retraumatising for a person and he may dissociate more as a consequence. A few considerations from my own experience may be helpful:

1. Recognising dissociation without judgment and without trying to overcome it, but rather looking for possible causes.

    Often, we think that 'spacing out', for example, is bad and we sometimes make efforts to be more present and alert. This is stressful and often counter-productive as it creates even more stress for our body. It is better to acknowledge what is happening and take it as a sign that something must be too much. As discussed before, dissociation shows up as an inability to feel, to move, to speak, to remember anything or to sense our body or parts of it. Even in ordinary life situations, we sometimes cannot remember a name or where we left our keys, but when we relax and forget all about trying to remember, suddenly the memory comes back by itself.

2. Connecting to present moment needs and resources, including social contacts.

Finding outer and inner resources is one of the principles of trauma healing and we will come back to this in Chapter Six. We often do not listen enough to the needs of our body and our heart, but are driven by desires and ambitions. Our eyes are focused on a future goal and the present moment is forgotten.

Remembering our needs in this moment, being more focused on them and what to do in order to satisfy those needs is an important art to learn. Sometimes relating with a friend or a person we feel close to also helps us to be more in the Here and Now and to feel loved and supported. As we will see, social engagement can be a way to regulate our energy and calm down.

3. Giving up analysing and intellectualising.

Prematurely trying to find a reason for why we are dissociated or overwhelmed is often an attempt to change a present state or to overcome it. It is therefore rooted in judgement and an effort to regain lost control. Real insights do not happen in this way, because they only come as a consequence of deep acceptance. Trauma means loss of control, and the wish to regain it is natural, but this can only happen after we have worked through layers of feelings and bodily sensations that are the result of certain past experiences.

4. Practicing various grounding and movement exercises, including self-touch.

Movement is a good way to come out of a dissociated state, especially involving legs, arms and face. Usually slow and contained movements work better. The focus should be on sensing the body and not on emotional discharge. When we learn to sense the periphery of the body, the constriction and charge that is often held at the core can expand and it becomes easier to handle. Also, self-touch and various hand postures can help a person to be present with bodily sensations.

Exercises

Stand on both legs. With your in-breath start to bend your knees slightly as you come down. With your out-breath come back up. Keep the rest of your body straight and relaxed as you continue to go down and come up in the rhythm of your breathing. Do this for some minutes and then stop in a position where your knees are slightly bent.

Now continue the same exercise, but this time also involve your arms. While breathing in let them swing backwards and while breathing out let them come back to its original position. Rest and observe what you notice in your body.

Sitting or standing, make a deep sound coming from your solar plexus. Let the mouth be open and let the deep sound come easily while breathing out. After some minutes allow your face muscles to also move, making some grimaces that come to you spontaneously. If you feel like it you can now include making movements with your whole body, together with the sound and the movements of the facial muscles. After a while rest and observe.

Sit and place one of your hands on your heart area and one on your belly. Then watch what is going on in your body.

Alternatively, you can place one hand on your heart and one on your forehead.

Or you can place one hand on your forehead and one hand behind your head as if you were holding your head with both your hands.

Keep your hands still and watch what is going on in your body.

5. Practicing how to tolerate and become more familiar with feelings that we usually avoid or reject (often negative feelings like anger, fear or pain).

When we learn to allow unwanted feelings consciously, even only slightly, the need to dissociate when these feelings arise is reduced. Healing trauma is only possible if we develop a certain capacity to tolerate unpleasant feelings and sensations without dissociating. This can be consciously practiced.

Besides the exercises mentioned above, it is possible to invent other exercises and playfully explore ways to handle emotions that are difficult for us or that we tend to avoid. I sometimes ask a client to practice every morning standing in front of a mirror and making an angry face or a monster face, just for 5 minutes, and then to stop and observe how this made him feel. In this way our body can learn to become comfortable with a certain expression rather automatically going into fear, resistance or judgement.

There are positive aspects to an unwanted emotion, and one can try to remember a moment in the past where that emotion served us in a positive way. Our life energy and strength are often hidden in rejected feelings and in the shadow side of our personality. It is certainly not easy to allow feelings that have overwhelmed us in the past without losing control, especially if they are related to a traumatic experience. It is therefore sometimes necessary to seek professional help.

Hints for helping others who are dissociated

It is a common mistake for therapists or helpers to confuse a dissociated state with a relaxed state of mind. As we discussed already, a dissociated state of body or mind is exactly the opposite of relaxation; it is a state of over activation and at the same time a disconnection from feeling that over activation. Relaxation, dissociation and also denial may appear similar and clients too are often confused about this. Sometimes dissociated states are mistaken for high states of consciousness. One may feel that one is capable of watching everything and not being identified with any emotions, but this might be just a very dissociated state.

The absent look in someone's eyes can be misunderstood as the emptiness of meditation. Arousal states are often easier to spot, while dissociation is more easily overlooked. It is usually much easier to recognise that a person red with anger, who declares that he is relaxed, is just in a state of denial than to recognise the dissociation in a person who outwardly appears calm and peaceful.

A therapist needs to be well regulated and connected to himself in order not to be pulled into the drowsiness and fog that a dissociated client often creates around himself. One may start to feel drowsy or sleepy oneself, and it takes experience and presence not to be affected by it.

Signs of dissociation can be a sleepy voice, too long gaps between words or sentences, an absent look or empty eyes, a slouchy body posture, the inability to remember something or make congruent sentences. Any element from the SIBAM may be missing in a person's expression, either the ability to sense the body, connect to feelings or an inability to move or make any sense of why something is happening. These signs can be subtler or very obvious, but a therapist needs to notice them and intervene accordingly. Otherwise the dissociation can become so profound that it may be difficult to help a person out of it.

Helpful considerations for therapists:

1. Observe body and vocal expression to differentiate relaxation from dissociation.

2. Watch for early signs of dissociation and possibly move away from exploring a trauma and instead resource a person and give support .

3. Accompany a person through a dissociated state by being present with them and give reassurance that you are there.

4. Speak with a clear voice without lengthy gaps and not in a hypnotic way.

5. Work with small body movements and exercises. Sometimes touch can be helpful too or asking the person to touch himself.

Dissociation basically indicates that a person is not ready to be confronted with a traumatic experience or that the degree of confrontation is too fast or too much.

The body gives clear indications and needs to be tracked carefully in order to prevent further disintegration.

Conclusion

To a certain degree, dissociation is a human condition and to come out of it is a sign of health and developing consciousness. In Zen it is said that an enlightened consciousness experiences ordinary life in an extraordinary way, while an unenlightened consciousness perceives life through layers of dust.

When a traumatised person is starting to reclaim the life energy that was frozen as a consequence of trauma he may see, hear, smell and sense all of life more fully. Suddenly, a tree appears greener than before, or a human touch will have a splendour that was never there before.

The fear of death

One of the topics that is usually ignored or avoided in our modern life is the fact that our time in this physical form is limited. Death is a subject that is usually never talked about; you will not find people at a dinner party discussing death. The strange thing is that even when people gather at funerals to give a send-off to a loved one, no one talks about death. Any other subject is discussed, but the most important one is avoided. The only certainty in life is the fact that we are going to die. We can't be certain whether anything else will happen or not, but death is absolutely certain.

And the way we deal with death is dissociation. We try to forget, we ignore, we postpone. Even people who have a terminal illness try to forget the fact that their time in this physical form is running out. It seems that the fear is overwhelming. Sometimes there are moments in life that remind us of our own death. That happens when a loved one dies or we encounter the near death of others. But we often respond to this reminder by denial or dissociation.

So, what should we do instead? The only meaningful approach is to start to encounter death, to meet our fears, to remind ourselves that death is always close by. It can happen at any moment. Carlos Castaneda writes in one of his books that a warrior lives with the awareness that death is always at his side. Osho said that a wise man will die before his physical death, so death cannot take anything away from him. And there are only two ways to die before we die, he explains: one is meditation and the other is love. Both are a death of the ego, of the illusory feeling that 'I' exist.

But before we manage that, we need to learn to face our fears. Dissociation is an escape from those fears. Woody Allan once said: "I am not afraid of death. I just do not want to be there when it happens." This is an accurate description of what dissociation means. It is an escape from fear and pain.

So, if dissociation is the symptom, then the cure will be to start dealing with those old fears that we have been avoiding in our lives: the fear of uncertainty, the fear of being left alone, the fear of survival, the fear of sex. Dissociation is not bad as such, but it does not allow us to process those wounds from our past. And it is the unprocessed fear and pain that blocks us from moving more deeply into life. Our lives are built around security, safety, certainty and they are all false, because essentially life is uncertain and insecure. In the mystical view, this is the very nature of life.

So, any event that brings us in touch with fear is a great opportunity to start a process of being with fear, experiencing deeply what it is and what it does to us. Only a full experience can become liberation and can bring an insight into the nature of fear. And that process is called meditation.

Meditation

Find a comfortable position and close your eyes. Let go into yourself as if you are falling inside. Imagine that you are losing all your energy, no energy to move or do anything at all.

Now let yourself remember that you are in this physical form only for a short time, you are just a guest on this planet for a little while. You come from afar and you will disappear one day into a vast emptiness.

Observe what happens in your body as you remind yourself of this fact. Do you feel any activation or do you tend to dissociate and drift away? Whatever happens do not judge or comment, simply notice it.

When fear comes up, remind yourself that right now in this moment you are here in this body. You are here to feel, sense and enjoy whatever life is presenting to you.

Now remember something that brings joy and happiness to your heart – a person or any event of your life, past or present.

Notice what you feel in your body right now as you remember that.

Take a few more minutes and then bring yourself

back by moving your body again.
You can record these instructions, allowing long enough gaps between the sentences and then listen to the recording while doing the meditation.

In order to be grounded and balanced we need to remember two things simultaneously: That we are going to die one day and also that we are alive right now in this very moment. If we forget one of these two aspects, we move out of balance and become lopsided.

This is one of my functions as a therapist: If a client is too fearful about death, I will remind him that he is alive right now and ask him what brings him joy and satisfaction in his life. If a person is too identified with his possessions, his achievements or relationships, I will remind him that one day he is going to lose it all. Life and death are like the two sides of one coin, they belong together. By remembering both, death and life, we can connect to our true reality.

Example from a session

A woman in her 30s is coming with the issue that she dissociates when in relationships. She tends to choose partners who live far away and before they separate from her, she usually leaves them. She is obviously trying to remain in control and avoid being overwhelmed by the fear of being left alone, which too much closeness or intimacy will bring up.
The root cause of her issue is with her mother who was unreliable in her childhood and the fear of losing her has not been processed. In the session she first learns to be present to feelings of fear without acting them out. She then also contacts the anger that she had

dissociated from in order not to risk annoying her mother. She more consciously starts recognising how afraid she was in her childhood of losing her mother, who was so unpredictable – a typical survival fear of children. Her need to bond with her mother was in conflict with her need to express and allow her true feelings.

In the session, she learns to allow her anger, consciously and gradually, to be there and, in this way, she can come out from her initial dissociation. She connects to courage and strength by allowing strong body sensations and a trembling and shaking of her whole body, something she had been holding back. Allowing these sensations and the physical release to pass through is part of her process of digesting and integrating her old childhood reactions. At the end she takes a deep breath and feels an expansion of her energy, a clear sign of having moved out of fear.

Relationship issues usually bring up unresolved bonding issues with our parents, which give us the opportunity to process and integrate them.

Chapter Three

Shame and Guilt

In this chapter, I will give a summarised understanding about shame and guilt, as they often appear in connection with trauma and can be long lasting aftereffects of a traumatic event.

First, it will be helpful to understand that shame and guilt are not part of our nature, but develop in a social context as they regulate the behaviour of the individual member of a social group. Besides this regulatory function that serves a collective system, there is also toxic shame and guilt that has a poisonous effect on our life and, after experiencing a traumatic event, we are especially susceptible to this. I will first mention the social function of shame and guilt and then examine its toxic effects and what is helpful to overcome it.

The social role of shame and guilt

Shame and guilt develop during our social upbringing and play an important role in all social systems to control the behaviour of its members. We are not born with these feelings, but they are passed on to us over generations – they are basically transgenerational. As a child grows up, he learns what his family and social environment appreciates or rejects, what is socially acceptable behaviour and what is not. The more we believe we must fulfil certain ideals and follow certain rules, the more shame or guilt we will experience if we fail to do so. Ideals and beliefs separate us from our natural self and create a division within us. This division is part of how a child is socialised and becomes a member of society. To a certain extent, it is necessary and is the way in which we are introduced to the world and society.

In the beginning, a child is wild, just like an animal and also feels oneness – no division exists in him. But this oneness is also unconscious and in the process of socialisation will have to be lost. So human beings become divided within themselves between their own natural self and what is expected of them by society and the world. The search to find that original oneness again in a conscious way is the spiritual journey.

In order to survive physically, a child is programmed by nature to bond and attach himself to his caretaker, which is mostly his mother in the beginning. This need to bond is the beginning of looking outside, originally to search for the mother, as we need her to survive. The attention becomes divided between feeling our own needs and what our mother wants from us. Following our mother's demands strengthens our attachment to her, but it separates us from our own needs, or at least it creates an inner split. As a child grows, this inner split grows too – it becomes our lifelong conflict between following our own inner nature or what our social surroundings expect from us.

These outer rules and values that we receive from our parents, teachers and other members of society eventually become inner voices that follow us throughout our life, and the feelings of shame and guilt tell us when we have overstepped a boundary and have gone against some internalised values and rules. This is called social conditioning.

The evolution of shame and guilt

Shame and guilt both developed in more highly evolved species of animals as they started to form social groups. Forming social bonds and respecting hierarchical order gave those animals a survival advantage over more primitive species. Social bonding served the survival of the whole group, including the individual. Being an outcast could be a death sentence for the individual group member, as it meant no one else would watch out for his welfare or share anything with him.

Shame is functionally designed to respect a system of social hierarchy; it helps to establish social order in a pack. Evolutionarily, this may be linked to the need for a subservient member to have automatic responses to the adult (male) leader. One can see the posture of shame in animals, when they concede to being inferior towards an animal of higher rank. It is like a feedback loop associated with a learning process, learning how to fit in socially. So, shame can be seen as an early instinctive force that develops in human infants as early as 15 months.

Guilt on the other hand is a later development and relates to the strengthening of the sense of belonging to a social group or family. It forms in children more clearly from age 3, when a child is more aware of the value system of the parents. A child tries to imitate a parental figure and if he fails to behave in tune with those values, he feels guilt and as a consequence tries hard to correct his behaviour. Through the sense of guilt, we form a collective conscience and a feeling of belonging to a group that will protect us against harm, and that we also will try to protect. This was evolutionarily important for foraging societies, where each individual had to rely on the others to survive disease, predators, and scarce resources.

So, one could say that shame relates more to the hierarchy within a group, while guilt is an indicator that gives members a sense of what is allowed or not allowed within the group to which they belong. It regulates and strengthens the sense of belonging.

While shame alerts us when we act in ways that may cause others to devalue us and not come to our aid, the guilt system is designed to detect if our action will endanger our belonging to the group, to stop such behaviour and take corrective action. In this way, natural selection favours those who feel guilt and shame. There is significant research suggesting that guilt and shame serve as an important adaptive function for human survival.

Differentiating between shame and guilt

There is a long discussion in scientific circles about the difference between guilt and shame, and their relative importance. In life, we often do not distinguish between the two and there are researchers who treat them as almost the same or say that guilt is only a subset of shame, but on the same continuum. Even though eventually we have to grow beyond the paralysing influence of these feelings, I believe it helps one's awareness to make a distinction.

Shame develops much earlier and relates more to who we are as a person; it relates to a time when the sense of self is not fully formed, making a child much more vulnerable to the judgment of others and their disapproving or diminishing gaze. In shame, it is not so much a question of what we have done, but of how we feel judged and devalued as a person and in our sense of self. As a consequence, we are more concerned with being found out than with amending our behaviour. The intensity of shame matches the degree to which we feel judged or devalued by someone who disapproves of us.

Guilt on the other hand is more concerned with what we have done and whether our action was inappropriate in a certain situation. That is why a guilty feeling often leads to an effort to correct our action and once we do that our guilty feeling is diminished. The intensity of guilty feelings is more linked to a person's internal values or the values he considers important.

When we feel shame, we condemn ourselves as being a bad person; we feel a painful deficiency as a person or self. This in turn often leads to passivity and a tendency to withdraw and give up. Guilt on the other hand seems to be more concerned with our actions. When we feel guilty, we are more likely to make amends and reparation for our actions and on the positive side may develop empathy for others. Shame on the other hand is characterised by withdrawal, hiding from the judgement of others and may lead to a sense of self-pity.

In some experimental studies, two-year-old children participated in a play session, during which a mishap occurred that the children appeared to have caused. Children who sensed more shame had a significant tendency to avoid the experimenter after the mishap and were slower to talk about it, while those who had more guilty feelings showed the opposite pattern. Their tendency was to tell the experimenter what had happened and make amendments for it.

It seems that in guilt we are more concerned about how we appear in our own eyes, which is why we can feel guilty even though no one knows about what we did. In shame, it is more a question of how we appear in the eyes of another; we are more concerned about being found out by someone else, which is why shame may lead to more transgressions and lying in order not to be devalued by others.

The development of toxic shame

Shame is a feeling we are often much less aware of than guilt and it is a subtle background feeling accompanying many of our actions. For example, we may not think that a person's need to show off is a behaviour based on shame, the shame of not being good enough. Shame develops early when our needs as a child are not met in an appropriate way over a long period of time. A child has the need to be protected and safe, the need to be loved and taken care of and the need to explore his environment and surroundings. As a child cannot talk, he is dependent on his mother or caretaker to be attuned to his needs and able to respond to them appropriately. When a baby cries, a mother who is attuned to the child, will know what his needs are. A mother whose own needs as a child were not responded to properly or who is traumatised will find it difficult to know and respond to her child's needs in an appropriate way.

In the beginning, when a mother does not fulfil the child's needs, he will protest, then he will get angry and sometimes even furious and eventually when all this does not lead to a fulfilment of his needs, he will give up, become 'quiet'. As he cannot go anywhere else to satisfy his needs, his only escape route is to shut down and dissociate; this dissociation, as we described before, is not the quietness of a relaxed fulfilment.

As a child has the urge to fulfil his needs, he is also programmed by nature to bond to his mother, as she is the one who is supposed to provide those needs. And when this fulfilment does not come from her, especially if this happens over longer periods of time, then he is suddenly in conflict between his own basic survival needs and his need to bond to his mother. In order not to lose contact with her, he will tend to give up his own basic needs, rather than feel that something is wrong with her. That sets the stage for toxic shame to develop.

Children cannot accept that something is wrong with their parents; they always tend to feel that something is wrong with themselves. And this is especially the case when parents are not able to acknowledge their children's needs for love, safety or exploration. They may say sentences like, "Don't be so needy. You are not a baby anymore", "Don't poke your nose into everything", "You never learn", "You are just like your father/mother", "If you continue like this, you will end up like your granddad."

Now whenever a natural need arises in the child, a feeling of shame comes with it. He feels that something is basically wrong with him, that he is incapable of doing anything properly or that he is basically a bad person. This shame develops because we believed that our parents or caretakers – who were not able to respond to our natural needs in a compassionate or understanding way – were, in fact, making a correct judgement about ourselves. In a way, shame is self-created – it is believing something that is untrue.

Parents often need to set limits to a young infant and say 'no' to what he intends to do. The question is whether they can still show empathy for the child or not. If they can, the child is not likely to develop a sense that he is wrong. But if they are not able to say 'no' with compassion, the child is more likely to develop a poisonous shame, a feeling that something is basically wrong with him as a person. People who grow up in abusive environments can easily get the message that they are undeserving, inadequate, and inferior; in other words, that they should feel ashamed of who they are.

Over time, intense feelings of shame can take hold of a person's self-image and create low self-esteem. One develops an overly strong concern about what other people think and may become super-sensitive to what feels like criticism, even if it isn't, and may easily feel rejected by others. Inside, one feels painful self-contempt and worthlessness.

Such core shame is the result of early psychological damage that impedes growth. In a more empathetic environment, we develop a reliable sense of self that in turn enables us to have a sense of guilt, which is more a sense of taking responsibility, and to view other people as separate and at the same time feel concern for them.

People who have been shamed often shame others later in life and those who feel high levels of shame have often been shamed early in life. This is also the way shame is transferred from one generation to the next. Instead of shaming others, a more constructive attitude would be to help someone to understand the effects of his actions on others and how he could take steps to make up for his transgressions.

The development of toxic guilt

While shame is a more complex emotion that according to scientific studies involves activation in larger parts of our brain, guilt is more connected to a person's learned social standards. In other words, guilt seems to be less destructive to our whole personality and also can be dealt with and overcome more easily. Toxic guilt has its base in toxic shame. We feel guilty when we transgress moral, ethical or religious norms and we criticise ourselves for it. This criticising, however, can become self-torturous and also originates from a time when we have been taught strict moral codes and standards. The stricter the rules and the more adamant our family or society was in imposing them, the more guilt we feel when we transgress those norms. A guilty feeling is like an inner alarm that tells us that now we are transgressing a rule or not behaving according to the values of our family or social group, and we may lose our right to belong there and will be condemned.

The more we feel the need to belong to the group, the more we are under the influence of guilt. For children, guilty feelings are hard to bear, because they feel so dependent on being approved of and loved by their parents. That is why children will in one way or another try to correct their behaviour and be in tune with their parents' values. Then their guilty feeling is reduced and a burden is lifted off their shoulders. Parents often consciously or unconsciously create guilty feelings in their children as a way to control their behaviour. One of the worst punishments is for a parent to say: "You are not my child anymore".

Evolutionarily guilt ties a group together and promotes the well-being of a social group by encouraging the individual to adhere to social conventions, but on the other hand it reduces a person's ability to behave in authentic, constructive and empathetic ways. In other words, a blind follower cannot feel real love; he can only do what his group expects from him. The degree of guilt that we feel often shows how important it is for us to belong to a particular social group.

The same action may give rise to feelings of shame and guilt, but the difference is that when we feel shame, we view *ourselves* in a negative light ("*I* did something terrible!"), whereas when we feel guilt, we view a particular *action* negatively ("I *did something terrible!*"). We feel guilty because our actions affected someone else, and we feel responsible. In a positive sense, this may lead to an attempt to make amends for our behaviour – we can say sorry or do something to 'pay our debts'. When we feel shame, this is more difficult as we cannot change who we are.

Guilt becomes toxic when it controls our life to such a degree that we cannot do anything that gives us authentic joy, as we feel so much under the control of social norms. It literally becomes difficult even to breathe. Strictly moral and also religious communities and societies create environments like this and anybody who steps out is deeply condemned and stigmatised. All natural impulses, in particular sexual impulses, become repressed. Guilt becomes part of social control and domination and can destroy a person's life and well-being. Christianity even teaches that man is born in sin, so it is not even a question of what you do, but from your birth you are already guilty.

Sometimes guilt is not tied to a specific event or personal behaviour, but we feel guilty about events over which we have no control. Then it can come out of a sense of feeling overly important and overly responsible, which is also something children feel as they go through the narcissistic developmental stage, during which they learn to develop their sense of 'I'. For example, children sometimes feel the storm came because they lied during the day and God is sending a punishment. Systemically, it can also be related to a hierarchical disorder, where a child tries to save a parent from a certain life destiny. We come back to this in the following chapter.

Guilt and trauma

People who survived a traumatic event, such as an accident or natural disaster while others did not, often experience a deep guilt that can stay with them long after the event. It is called 'survivor guilt' and there is dissent in scientific circles about how much this relates to actual guilt or to shame or to both.

But with any traumatic event it is likely that feelings of shame or guilt come up, particularly if we blame ourselves for what happened. The mind can revolve in endless circles about what we could or should have done differently and how we could have prevented what happened. Our response depends on whether our personality is more shame or more guilt based, and also on the specific kind of trauma we are facing. To varying degrees, a sense of guilt or self-blame can impair our ability to function.

It could be that a woman who has been abused believes that it was her own fault that the perpetrator was attracted to her. It could be that a holocaust survivor is tortured by thoughts about why it was he who survived and not his friend. It could be that after a car accident someone judges himself for not having paid more attention and responding more quickly to the car coming from the right. Or we may feel guilty for not completing a relationship with a loved one who died. Even in small situations, for example if we cannot find our car keys, there are people who blame themselves excessively for such details and one can imagine how much this negative attitude towards oneself may be multiplied in the case of a real traumatic event. Whether we respond with shame or guilt largely depends on early childhood hang-ups.

In my experience, after Meera's accident, I felt much guilt on various levels. I felt so guilty that I had taken her on that holiday, that I did not take care for her more by double checking the dive cylinder, or for not staying closer to her on that dive. I literally felt as though I had killed her, that I was responsible for her accident and for not saving her life. It was a torturous feeling that returned to me many times for months to come. And nothing that came from my intellect or from other people's comments could change how I felt inside.

My feeling of guilt could be triggered by almost anything. I felt terrible that I could not arrange a more beautiful celebration for her, that I could not manage to stay with her body all the time or prevent the autopsy of the doctor. I felt sorry for her and myself. How could the worst possible event happen in the worst possible place on earth? Why at such a moment and in such a place? I was all alone there with no support and everything was plain, primitive and not worthy for honouring my wife's departure from this life.

I took responsibility for almost everything. I felt so utterly helpless and hopeless and alone as I had never felt before in my entire life. And I just wanted to disappear with her. Why did this happen to her and not to me? I had guilt attacks that would come sometimes like a big wave, where I just wanted to hit my head against a wall. It seems to me that only the pure necessity of having to take care of practical matters forced me out of such states.

Looking back, I am still amazed at how I managed to function and arrange for many things that even in a normal situation would be intense. I guess it was only possible because I was in an altered state with a high level of dissociation. The number of endorphins in my system allowed my intellect to function well enough to make practical decisions and not become overwhelmed by emotions. The high adrenalin rush in my blood kept me going with almost no sleep and the periodical emotional outbursts allowed enough discharge of energy, so my system could release certain tensions. Also, I guess, my years of meditation and being with a Master helped me to remind myself and view death not as a calamity, even if on an emotional and biological level it was.

Over the coming months, I practiced just to allow all my feelings, thoughts and sensations to happen without trying to do anything about them, not trying to control, postpone or make them less, but just letting happen whatever wanted to happen at any moment, not caring about what others may think when suddenly in a train or on the street my tears would start to flow and consume me. Maybe this helped me to slowly come out of the dissociated state.

Often our minds will find endless reasons why we are guilty or responsible in one way or another. We actually may have real responsibilities for something that happened, or have really made mistakes in responding to a situation. We may discover later in what way we were not aware or present and therefore contributed to the event. But this is not the point. It is the overwhelming, uncontrollable sense of guilt or shame that can be so torturous. The mind continues in a compulsive way to repeat the same thoughts in a useless attempt to gain control and rewrite the history of a past chain of events. It can be a combination of guilt and helplessness that is fuelled by hyper arousal, but can often leave a person in depression and without energy.

It is helpful to learn to acknowledge and accept such feelings as part of a response to trauma and find a way for the body to discharge its activation. Just as when dealing with other symptoms, one needs to process the grief and pain and all other feelings with compassion and love. It also is important to develop a meditative awareness and an understanding that we are all part of a cosmic drama, in which we play a certain part and we are not in control of that.

Healing Shame

Sometimes excessive shame can be an indication that there has been either abuse or neglect in the past or some other early trauma. As mentioned above, children tend to blame themselves rather than their parents to protect their attachment bond. For healing shame, it is therefore important to examine and heal the relationship to one's parents and learn to see them as the people they really are, neither idealising nor demonising them. We will discuss this more in Chapter Five.

As shame has its base in an early mis-attunement to a child's basic needs, the first step in healing shame is to acknowledge and accept those needs as natural, to feel compassion for oneself and for the child that we once were. It is about giving to yourself what your parents were not able to give you. In a further step, we then need to identify those beliefs that gave rise to feelings of shame and question their truth. Wrong beliefs and identifications that we still cling to do not allow us to fully feel our authentic needs.

In shame, a child is concerned about losing the love and connection to a parental figure, because he did something wrong. He develops an oversensitivity about not making any mistakes, and as a result does not allow himself to follow his own explorative impulses and tends to withdraw, hoping to avoid any conflict. In the healing of shame, it is therefore important to learn what one's impulses and needs are, even if they cannot always be fulfilled. One needs to learn to develop a healthy sense about one's own and other people's boundaries.

Shame often leads to a freezing of our life energy and when we slowly come back from the freeze strong emotions can emerge and we need to be prepared to deal with them. These are sometimes the feelings that we repressed as a child, like resignation and helplessness, rage and protest, but also the fear of losing our parents' affection. Allowing such feelings, especially any repressed anger, can be helpful in providing us with the necessary energy to move through and out of shame and find authentic joy.

Physiologically, shame on one hand, and joy, confidence or pride on the other hand relate to different, quite opposite body postures, which is why it is impossible to feel ashamed and at the same time joyful, self-confident or proud. Discovering the healthy aggression underneath feelings of shame and helplessness will activate our life force, which can instantly change our body posture, move us out of shame and connect us to feelings of joy. Now it is easier to identify those old beliefs and identifications that made us feel ashamed. Joy is the best antidote to shame.

Sometimes rage or hate can also be a way of compensating and avoiding feelings of shame. For example, a person can show a false pride or assertiveness or can shame others. Rather than being shamed again, one makes others ashamed. In such situations, it is important to first uncover the original shame that drives such behaviour before one can feel the more authentic emotions underneath.

Dealing with shame can be tricky, as the simple awareness of shame can make a person feel more ashamed, which can lead to a negative cycle where shame gets reinforced and one feels shame for feeling shame! A person may notice that he gets red in the face and that makes him feel even more ashamed. This is the reason why, for a therapist to mention a client's shame or worse, to even mention that he does not need to feel ashamed, may not be a very helpful intervention. Making the client aware of any hidden anger may be a better approach – or finding something that makes the client feel proud of himself.

Meditative awareness further helps to loosen the identification with shame. Rather than becoming one with shame, one learns to sense it and move into it and out of it. Like any other feeling it is time limited.

Healing Guilt

To overcome toxic guilt, we first need to learn to be centered and grounded in the present, be mindful of our body and respectful of our feelings and adult needs. It is good to recognise and allow the feelings and needs of the child that we once were and that still lives inside, but it is not helpful to become identified with it. Only from an adult space can we give up the attachment to our parents and learn to tolerate the guilty feelings of the child that may arise as a consequence of not living according to their values and rules. The adult can learn to feel okay to be an outsider and only then develop his own and different set of values. Then feelings of guilt can slowly give way to feelings of joy. It was the need of the child to belong to his family and be safe that made him give himself up in order to be loved. By realising one's capacity to be alone and find one's own creativity and life path, one grows into being mature and adult.

There are other guilty feelings that are more related to interpersonal relating. For example, when our actions have hurt someone, we may also have guilty feelings. To empathise with that person's pain and to feel remorse for having caused it are all signs of emotional health. When we make amends for our behaviour, our guilty feeling is usually reduced. Such feelings serve empathetic interpersonal relationships and we need to distinguish them from toxic guilt.

Sometimes a sense of guilt will remain, as we cannot always fully make amends for our actions. Then we need to carry the guilt and let it become part of our life and this in return will contribute to our inner strength and maturity. There is a difference between guilty feelings and guilt. Guilty feelings indicate that we have not yet made amends for a hurtful action, while guilt is a result of recognising and accepting the consequences of our actions. It is more like responsibility. If I hurt someone badly, I may have to agree to the consequence that my relationship with this person is over, even if I make amends for what I did, or say that I am sorry. This can be painful, especially if we had a strong attachment to the person.

Sometimes we try to escape this pain and want to change what happened or want to undo it, which is never possible. Or we behave like a child and want the other to relieve us of the guilt or responsibility, so we can feel better. A feeling of guilt after a traumatic event can be difficult for a person to bear. One may have killed another person in an accident and the feeling of guilt may stay there one's whole life, as no action can change the fact of what happened and bring the person back. But this is not the same as the guilty feeling that comes when we are not taking responsibility. Accepting guilt and being able to carry it is a sign of maturity and eventually gives us strength.

Learning to be open to the feelings of pain and sorrow for what happened and becoming conscious of what exactly one's guilt is – and what it is not – takes awareness and is often not easy. Sometimes we carry a guilt that does not belong to us, which we often see in family systems, and then we make ourselves overly important. On the other hand, there is a guilt we need to accept and carry together with our family as part of our life's destiny. When we take too much responsibility, we make ourselves too big and play the hero and this does not lead to strength, but to a collapse of our life energy. When we deny any guilt, we lose connection and grounding and remain immature.

Personally, I still feel in a process of disentangling myself from those strong feelings of guilt, where I take too much responsibility for something that was beyond me. On the other hand, I need to admit to my own acts of unconsciousness and feel the pain that this can create for myself and sometimes for others. The severe consequences of that obviously cannot be changed and I have to bear them.

Spiritual guilt

I also want to mention another kind of guilt that is not created by society or social upbringing. It is not guilt towards someone, but towards oneself. It arises when our consciousness grows and we feel that there is something more to life and we are not working hard enough to get to it, but waste our time. This spiritual guilt is very meaningful. Unless we have reached to our highest peak of consciousness, there will be a sense of guilt for not living up to our real potential and a feeling that we create suffering for ourselves and those who are in contact with us. Feeling this guilt is meaningful and essential as it gives us motivation and determination and supports our spiritual search.

Exercises

1. *Write down or share with another person how you are related to your feelings and needs. Which ones are easy for you to feel or express and which ones you are more likely to hide or repress? Which feelings or needs do you feel ashamed of or are afraid of? Do you know the difference between*

needs and desires and how do you react when some are not fulfilled?

2. *Identify some beliefs and ideas about yourself that you have picked up from your parents. Say such a sentence loud to yourself and observe what happens in you and in your body. Examine if you feel this is a true statement or not.*

3. *Make a list of things that you like and appreciate about yourself and that you feel proud of.*

Example from a session

Mike is coming to a session because he feels that his life is in a downward spiral. His job is not working well and he feels ashamed that he is not getting anything together and feels like a failure. He also feels guilty for having left his wife just a year after they had a child together and does not know how to heal the relationship with her.

In the session we start exploring his feelings of shame by examining his family background. His parents separated when he was a teenager and, in a constellation set up, we can see his mother turning away from the rest of the family. It becomes clear that his mother is carrying some destiny related to her own original family, which does not allow her to see her child and partner (he reports that she also does not want to speak about her own family). I explain to him that a child usually tends to think that something is wrong with him, when a mother is not available. In the work, he realises that his mother's inability to see him and attend his needs as a child is caused by her own family background, likely by a trauma in her original family.

He feels greatly relieved of shame and now, with more compassion, can recognise his unfulfilled needs from childhood, honour the neglect he had to go through and find ways to attend his present-day needs.

In a second step, he learns that one reason he left his wife was to show himself what a useless person he is. It is a re-enactment of his childhood trauma. After seeing this, he now becomes able to acknowledge his true responsibility and guilt towards his wife and child without blaming himself and this in turn gives him the strength to now take appropriate action.

Meditation

Sit comfortably and close your eyes. Remember a situation or event where you feel you behaved in a way that you regretted later and that made you feel guilty or ashamed. Notice what happens in you and in your body as you remember this. What feelings come up and what goes on in your mind.

Now inwardly or loudly say 'yes'. Yes, I did this. Open yourself to the fact that this is exactly what you did and something in you wanted to do things in this way. Imagine you are looking at a big force or feel a big force from behind that moves you even against your wishes. Make yourself available to that force and repeat the word 'yes'.

Do this for a few minutes and then observe what happens inside you.

Collective shame and guilt

Collective shame or guilt is a consequence not of a personal experience, but because we feel part of a family or social group or country. Then the guilt or shame we feel is not related to our own action, but they arise because of what our family members or even our ancestors have done. We feel a certain shared responsibility that is a consequence of our sense of belonging. There is a saying 'cling together, swing together' that accurately describes how the bonding to our family or social group compels us to carry a responsibility or sense of guilt that in reality belongs to someone else.

A child whose father has committed crimes knowingly or unknowingly will have a sense of guilt and will want to atone for his father's acts. A woman whose family became rich by exploiting people in the past may unconsciously reject her inherited riches and continually lose her money. Descendants of a murderer may feel an unconscious pull towards committing suicide. The descendant of a woman who gave all her children up for adoption may open a home for orphans.

The work of Family Constellation offers endless examples of how we not only carry guilt for close family members, but sometimes for ancestors belonging to previous generations and how we are compelled to balance their deeds.

Trans-generational shame or guilt is often connected to collective trauma and we will discuss this in more detail in Chapter Four.

More Examples from sessions

An Indian man who lives and was born in Kenya and whose forefathers came from India has a deep sense of shame and unworthiness. In the session it comes out that he was bullied as a child for being Indian (personal experience of feeling shamed) and also, he carries the collective shame for his family members that feel closely bonded to India and carry the sense of inferiority at being under British rule.

A Turkish man living in Germany feels deep shame in his work and never allows any feelings of anger in himself. The session reveals that his grandparents had to escape from a civil war in a Balkan country and had to start a new life in Turkey, still remaining outsiders there and feeling the loss of their home. He copies their experience of being far from home and an outsider, and the feeling of not being wanted. He also carries the repressed anger that refugees often feel and have to hold back in order to survive in their new place.

Chapter Four

Bonding and Collective Trauma

Since the spread of Family Constellation in therapeutic circles throughout the world there has been a growing understanding about the importance of collective and systemic trauma. There are traumatic events that affect a whole family, a whole nation or even a whole culture. Since World War II, it has become more evident how a collective group can be affected by the suffering of their ancestors from previous generations. For example, the descendants of those who were tortured or victimised in the past may carry a feeling of wanting revenge. Or the descendants of perpetrators carry a deep sense of guilt that they seek to atone for in their lives. Through bonding, one can feel directly involved in the events that happened to a previous generation without any direct personal experience. This goes even far beyond the secondary developmental trauma that a child experiences when his traumatised mother cannot properly attend to his needs.

 The systemic work of Family Constellation has brought a wider view on how this occurs, and in order to comprehend it more fully we need to understand what bonding is and how it affects us as individuals. I will give a short summary here about this important aspect of human interaction because relationships can exist with or without strong bonding, but also bonding can exist outside any close relationship.

The power of bonding

Every human being is born into a family field and is programmed to instinctively bond and connect to his primary caretaker, which in most cases is his mother. This is a powerful survival arrangement by nature, which needs a child to survive and be taken care of. A human child is amongst the most helpless creatures in the world and this situation lasts for many years. It has been said that in a way a child is born prematurely. In order to make sure that this child is taken care of, nature creates a strong bond between the child and his parents – in particular between the child and his mother.

For this close relationship to form, a baby is instinctively more interested in a human face than anything else, and in particular in human eyes. To support the creation of a strong bond towards the primary caretaker, the child also needs to learn to distinguish who is its mother and who is not. Gradually, the child will learn to distinguish his mother's face from the face of others, which is the time when children develop stranger anxiety. So along with bonding comes the capacity to make a separation between one person and another. While bonding brings us together with some people, it simultaneously also separates us from others.

This attachment is mutual and also comes from the side of the mother. She will be attuned to the needs of her child if she herself is not severely traumatised and was able to develop a strong and healthy bond to her own mother. The strength of the attachment can be seen in the stress and pain that is immediately apparent when there is a disruption or separation between mother and child. The child becomes restless, begins to cry or scream, which creates an impulse in the mother to attend to her child. The intensity of this stress reaction depends on the age of the child, the length of the separation from the mother and on the child's previous experience with his mother, whether or not the mother has been reliable and present in the past.

Attachment behaviours have been studied extensively by John Bowlby, who described how typically a child first responds upon separation with fear or panic, then with anger and rage and eventually with despair and apathy. Mary Ainsworth, a colleague of Bowlby, in her later research discovered various relating patterns based on how children respond to their mothers upon separation and reunion. She distinguished between different bonding styles that children develop according to their previous bonding experience with their mother. She called them secure and insecure attachment styles, and divided the latter into three sub-groups, ambivalent (or anxious), avoidant and disorganised. As the child grows up, this becomes a pretty consistent way of relating to others in adult life. As there is extensive literature about this topic, I will not go into further details here.

It is important to acknowledge that a disturbance in early bonding is at the root of many psychological and psychosomatic problems. Even though we form bonds to other family members and to others later in life, the bonding to our mother remains the most significant. Attachment to the mother is already formed before birth and creates a foundation for the healthy development of brain structures. One could call this mother child bonding 'biological love', because it is partly instinctive and not our choice or decision. It is nature's way of helping a child survive and thus to secure the continuation of our species. Therefore, it is a very powerful force. Even though bonding takes different forms, the wish to bond or the wound of an unfulfilled need to bond will accompany us throughout our entire life.

We later also form bonds to our father, to siblings and other members of the family. Eventually we form bonds to friends, lovers, and partners, but the bond to our original family seems to remain strongest, probably because it relates to an unconscious sense that we need our family in order to survive.

Bonding between partners

In general, the strength of a bond depends on many factors: how important a person is to us, how much exchange there is between us, previous bonding experiences and also if sexual contact is involved or not. As bonding is the biological aspect of love, sexual contact tends to create such a bond. If there is also love, then the strength of the bond increases. And the more exchange and mutual sharing there is in a relationship, the further the sense of bonding between the partners increases. The strength of this bond can be felt in the pain we experience when the relationship ends. Sometimes people are afraid of this pain and therefore keep the exchange to a minimum. They maintain their sense of freedom to do what they want and the relationship remains poor. Many people confuse this kind of freedom with the authentic freedom that only arises with love.

So, eventually our learning is to let our sense of freedom rise above the mundane freedom of being able to do whatever we want, which is a desire and comes from the mind, and simultaneously to let our love grow beyond the bonding love that is simply a desire to be together, towards a higher love that arises from our inner being. Growing beyond bonding is a lifelong task and not easy. It happens when we grow beyond the identification with our body and mind. A good practice might be to drop ideas such as 'my' partner, 'my' child, 'my' mother, 'my' body and try to give up such possessiveness.

Meera was my life partner and for 25 years we had shared our lives very intimately and a deep resonance had grown between us, where we could feel the other even when we were not physically together. When Meera suddenly left, it was such a shock that I felt as if a part of me had died and suddenly disappeared. I just wanted to go with her. Nothing in life mattered to me anymore and I had this deep feeling of wanting to be in her place instead of staying on this shore. For many weeks I acted as if in a trance like state and whenever I went to bed in the evening I was lying down on my back as if I were a dead corpse. The only moments I felt alive was when I was allowing my tears to flow and could cry without control.

In a relationship, you give to the other and receive from the other and when your partner dies or suddenly leaves, there is a feeling that a part of you has also left, that everything the other gave you is flowing back to her. As a consequence, you may feel as if half of you is no longer there. This may be one of the reasons why often when one partner in a lifelong relationship dies in old age, the other dies quite soon afterwards. The bond and attachment are so strong that one wants to follow the other.

Bonding is like a deep magnetic force that pulls us towards someone. It is healthy, life affirmative and part of our capacity as humans is to be able to surrender to such a force. But to remain under its influence is also limiting, as it also creates separation and duality, and prevents us from being open to the whole. Bonding is also the cause of conflict and even wars. We may identify with the people from our group and take revenge in their name without considering if we have any right to do so. To form relationships is our human capacity, but not the ultimate goal of life, rather a first lesson to learn about relating and feel connected to the whole.

We come into this life hard-wired by nature to live in a vast social field and form various relationships and attachments to others. These social relationships affect the way we feel, think and behave and have profound influences on our physical and psychological health. However, this ability to bond can be impaired as a result of trauma, whether developmental or because of shock. In order to grow beyond bonding, this original capacity needs to be 'repaired'.

Collective bonding

Besides bonding to an individual, we also form bonds to social groups. As mentioned, the most important one is our original family and that includes members from past generations. Family Constellation as a method has been particularly revealing about how family members of past generations belong to the relational field of our family and can continue to have astonishing influences on our behaviour, our feelings and our whole life. This means that bonding is not limited to the people we consciously know, but we also bond to others from past generations that we have never personally met or seen. In particular, these are family members who had a special life destiny or traumatic experience. It can even include non-relatives with whom our parents or grandparents created strong bonds. In the following chapter I will describe how a constellation shows which members of our extended family are strongly impacting us, often without our conscious awareness.

On a deep unconscious level, there seems to exist a collective matrix or energy field that binds families, members of a culture, religion or country together and this energy works equally on all those who belong to that group. Under its influence, we take over the feelings of others, we feel guilty for the deeds of people we do not know personally, we are driven to act on behalf of those who are already dead and may take revenge for atrocities that did not happen to us.

Without understanding the power of bonding, this may seem inexplicable. Systemic constellation is a method that reveals the energy of bonding and shows how we are simultaneously influencing such an energy field and are also influenced by it. This helps us to become aware of how and to whom we are bonded and with whom we identify on an unconscious level. The people we feel closest to are not necessarily the ones who have the strongest influence on our behaviour, our feelings and our way of thinking. We will discuss this more in the following chapter.

Belonging to a family, a partner, a political group, a religious or spiritual group, a company or association, or a country gives us a sense of identity and safety.

Knowing where we belong, identifying with certain beliefs and creeds, attaching ourselves to those who are important to us seems to give us strength and stability in a changing world. It provides us with a false sense of knowing who we are. We all know how people, for example at informal gatherings like a dinner party, try to find out what your profession is, where you come from, whether you have your own family and so on.

The need to belong is often at the root of many of our major life decisions, whether it concerns relationships or work. Someone may decide to move to another country without being aware that he is living out the longing of his father who was an immigrant and was forced to leave his original motherland. Or one may marry someone belonging to a family from the opposite side after a civil war, not knowing that one is unconsciously trying to heal a collective wound and promote peace between the two sides.

"There are some experiments conducted by Henry Tajfel at Bristol University, which produced unexpected results. Parties of schoolboys aged fourteen to fifteen were subjected to a quick, and bogus, psychological test; then each boy was told that he was either a 'Julius person' or an 'Augustus person'. No explanation was given about the characteristics of the Julius or Augustus people, nor did the boys know who the other members of their group were. Nevertheless, they promptly identified with their fictitious group, proud to be a Julius person or an Augustus person to such an extent that they were willing to make financial sacrifices to benefit their anonymous group brothers and to cause discomfort to the other camp.

Tajfel says that you can predictably alter a person's behaviour just by telling him he belongs to a group – even a group which he has never heard of before. Almost automatically the participant in these experiments favours anonymous members of his own group and, given the opportunity, is likely to go out of his way to put members of another group at a disadvantage. People will stick up for a group to which they happen to be assigned, without any indoctrination about who else is in the group or what its qualities are supposed to be."

(This is a quote taken from Uniyo Mystica Vol I #10, by Osho)

And further:

"Arthur Koestler relates these experiments to a childhood episode of his own.

On my first day at school, aged five, in Budapest, Hungary, I was asked by my future classmates the crucial question: 'Are you an MTK or an FTC?' These were the initials of two leading soccer teams, perpetual rivals for the league championship, as every schoolboy knew – except little me, who had never been to a football match. However, to confess such abysmal ignorance was unthinkable, so I replied with haughty assurance: MTK, of course!

And thus the dice was cast: for the rest of my childhood in Hungary, and even when my family moved to Vienna, I remained an ardent and loyal supporter of MTK; and my heart still goes out to them, all the way across the Iron Curtain. Moreover, their glamorous blue-and-white striped shirts never lost their magic, whereas the vulgar green-and-white stripes of their unworthy rivals still fill me with revulsion.

I am even inclined to believe that this early conversion played a part in making blue my favourite colour. After all, the sky is blue, a primary colour, whereas green is merely the product of its adulteration with yellow. I may laugh at myself, but the emotive attachment, the magic bond, is still there, and to shift my loyalty from the blue-white MTK to the green-white FTC would be downright blasphemy."

We pick up our allegiances like infectious germs and are mostly unaware of how these predilections run our lives, our preferences and more importantly are the origin of many historic disasters and hostilities.

One needs to be aware of the essential difference between authentic love and bonding. Bonding is an unconscious pull that may appear like love, but actually is more related to our need to belong to a group in order to survive and feel safe. Authentic love only arises when we become capable of loosening those bonds and can stand alone, like an outsider.

Bonding is important for a child's survival and because of our need for safety.

The ability to bond and relate to others gives us strength; it helps us to sustain a relationship even in times of difficulty. It therefore contributes to our physical and psychological health and makes us resilient against trauma and other life challenges. But remaining under the influence of the need to belong is also a cause of war, and of hostility towards those whom we want to keep out of what we consider to be the property of our group. In other words, what was helpful and necessary at the beginning of our life becomes a problem and limitation later on. Until we learn to loosen the influence of bonding on our lives, we are still run by the blind forces of instinctive nature.

The development of conscience

The mother-child bond is originally physical; after all, the child comes out of the body of his mother. Bonding also helps to release hormones and chemicals that encourage rapid brain growth. Along with the development of the brain comes the rapid development of the emotional and mental life of a child, so bonding affects many areas of life. A child starts to imitate his mother in many ways, her way of feeling and acting and eventually her way of speaking and thinking. A child starts to pick up all the attitudes and values of his mother and later of others in the family. Imitation or assimilation is the first and most primitive way of learning and it strengthens the bonding a child feels and his sense of belonging to his mother and whole family. What the mother likes and appreciates, the child will learn to like and appreciate. His whole personality structure develops around values that he absorbs from his environment and those who are closest to him.

In the beginning, a child has no sense of good or bad or right or wrong, so in a way everything is equal for him. Spiritually speaking, one could say he comes from a space of oneness where all is divine, and all is good. And this is so even in pain or discomfort. A child in pain is totally at one with the pain; nothing else exists in that moment. That is why children are always beautiful in the way they express things. They are total and whole. But this wholeness is unconscious, which is why they are going to lose it. They learn the ways of the world, which is the way of duality, right and wrong, good and bad, beautiful and ugly. In other words, a child learns values. Originally these values come from the parents and later from other members of society. The thinking mind develops within the child, which is a reflection of the world he lives in. And thinking means dividing, the feeling of wholeness is lost.

Shakespeare: "Nothing is good or bad. Only thinking makes it so."

As a child learns what his mother likes and dislikes, what pleases and what displeases her, he learns to listen to something outside of himself rather his own inner impulses. This strengthens their bond and his sense of belonging, but it also divides him. From this moment on, a growing conflict begins about whether to follow what he wants or what his mother would like. As he becomes more aware of his mother's preferences the question arises more and more strongly: Is what he wants to do agreeable to his mother or not? This is how a child starts to move away from his own organic oneness. From now on, a growing split and lifelong conflict occurs between his need to bond to others, his need to belong and his need to follow his own impulses – his need for freedom.

According to many psychologists, when there is healthy bonding early in life, there is also a natural movement towards self-realisation, maturity and individuation. However, when there has been no appropriate response to the child's need to bond – for example, in the case of trauma – then this can lead to attachment difficulties. There is a lot of research about insecure attachment and its consequences for healthy relationships later in life. In such cases, the conflict between the need to bond and the need to trust oneself remains unresolved.

At the same time, as the mind develops and begins to absorb values from outside, a conscience is growing inside. Unlike consciousness, conscience always relates to values; it is an inner force that tells us what is right and what is wrong. It is the internalised voice of our parents and of society. We can sometimes actually hear this inner voice telling us what we should or should not do.

When a child has a 'good' conscience and feels innocent, it usually means that his behaviour is in accordance with the values of his social environment, his parents and family. If he has a 'bad' conscience on the other hand, or feels guilty, this means that he did – or is about to do – something that is not in accordance with those values. The guilty feeling is urging him to correct his behaviour and until he does, it will stay with him. It reminds him that he may not be considered a 'good' child anymore and may be in danger of being excluded or sent away. Such feelings have their roots in our most archaic fears, where being excluded threatened our very survival.

The influence of conscience

This is the way we all learn how to be a 'good' child, a 'good' student, a 'good' husband or wife, a 'good' citizen. It is called conditioning: learning the values of our family and social surroundings. It may be enforced from the outside at the beginning, but then it becomes internalised and takes the form of a conscience and one starts to feel as if this is one's own inner voice. Osho used to call conscience 'the inner policeman'. One of the most important things to learn on a spiritual path is how to distinguish the voice of conscience from one's own inner voice, one's authentic and natural impulses.

Going against one's conscience, against the values of one's family or society is frightening. It sometimes feels as if we are dying, because it triggers the survival fear that is at the source of our need to belong. It is the reason why people often remain in miserable life situations, because at least they do not feel alone, they keep a sense of being part of a group or society. They do not need to face guilty feelings or a bad conscience. Only individuals who have the courage to tolerate such feelings and are ready to stand alone, without being bothered by the opinions of others, have a chance for spiritual development and can grow their own consciousness that is beyond conscience. In other words, development means learning to loosen the influence of bonding, the biologically driven impulse to belong, and enter a space of authentic love that comes out of one's ability to be alone.

We can sometimes have a taste of these moments of innocence, of being undivided, for example when we are totally absorbed and immersed in something we are doing or when melting with someone in love or in meditative moments. When there is no sense of 'I', we can have a glimpse of that original state of non-duality we were born with. It is like a return or homecoming.

But before this can become our reality, we will have to deal with the force of conscience that accompanies us throughout our life. In each relationship, in each social context, we develop a certain conscience that, just like a barometer, tells us if we are in danger of losing our right to belong. The strength of this force depends on how important it is for us to belong to this social group or to stay in that relationship. Conscience always relates to values that are valid in a particular group or relationship. These values are relative and vary from group to group or relationship to relationship. What is considered sin in one religion may be considered virtue in another. What my mother likes, my father may hate. What one of my friends may consider beautiful, another friend may view as vulgar. So, our conscience is a continual source of conflict; there is no way to have peace of mind. Peace of mind does not exist, because mind divides and that is the source of conflict and tension.

We learn not only to strengthen our sense of belonging, but we also learn to separate ourselves from others who do not belong or should not be allowed to belong to 'our' group, to 'our' family. We may even exaggerate small differences between us and those 'others' just in order to keep them clearly divided and secure our own place in our group. This serves the same biological will to survive. It is a deep imprint in our unconscious and is at the root of many conflicts and wars between countries, religions, cultures and social groups. It is the reason why immigrants sometimes refuse to mix with a new culture and prefer to suffer rather than to give up an old identity, even exaggerating outdated rituals and traditions in order to keep their sense of belonging alive.

Just as children bond to their parents, people bond to a country, a religion, a culture, and fear that without it they are in danger of being annihilated and overrun. This fear may grip anyone who lives in a foreign country or culture, or is faced with the issue of giving up an old identity and opening to a new life situation.

All over the world we can see this tendency to hold on to an old, familiar tradition. It gives the mind a sense of certainty, peace, safety, and belonging and at the same time it excludes those 'others', who have to be kept away.

Exercise

Use a piece of paper to write this down or share with a partner.
Remember a past moment in your life, whether recently or from childhood, where you had a bad conscience and felt guilty towards someone else. Remember the feelings and thoughts that came with it. How did you respond and what eventually helped you to cope with it?

Beyond conscience

In my first book, *The Roots of Love*, I have described how conscience is a social phenomenon that gives us a sense of belonging to a group or family and also a place within that family. It gives us a place within time and space. It is the way the human mind structures reality, but at the same time it keeps us within the boundaries of the mind. Conscience is a mind phenomenon that keeps us confined; it is a substitute for a missing consciousness.

One of the first things to learn in order to develop one's consciousness as a human being is to practice being an outsider. Only an outsider can have the freedom to develop his own values, understanding and intelligence that are not part of the mass mind. In the beginning, this is often accompanied by a feeling of guilt or the sense of doing something wrong. One may be judged or laughed at and may face a feeling of loneliness, emptiness and fear. If one is capable of tolerating these feelings without trying to get rid of them, one will gradually be less dominated by conscience and become more able to develop one's own individuality and a deeper sense of personal priorities, that is less a result of social conditioning.

Osho often reminded his disciples that wanting to be 'good' in any area of life is the wrong goal. Whether it is to be a good parent, a good husband or wife, a good teacher, a good therapist or a good citizen, does not matter. The more one tries to be good, the more one moves away from oneself and adheres to the values of others. This is not the way to become fulfilled, but only to feel discontented, which is why one often sees 'good' people suffering. It seems only the so-called 'bad' people enjoy life, because they care less about the opinion of others.

Sometimes we deceive ourselves and create another group of outsiders, of avant-garde people, to which we now want to belong – and the same game continues. We now want to adhere to values opposite to those of mainstream society, but our desire to belong has not changed at all. We are in the same trap as before, just imagining we are out of it.

The only real way to move beyond conscience is meditation, moving beyond mind and discovering that there is no need to belong anywhere, because we already belong to the whole of life. Once we have glimpses of this truth as an existential experience, we have started to move beyond bonding. Practicing how to be relaxed and alert when feeling like an outsider can be a good preparation.

Meditation: Expand in all directions

Close your eyes and imagine yourself expanding in all directions. Begin in your heart and start to dissolve all the walls and boundaries you have created around yourself. Remember that life is always uncertain and insecure and all the safety measures we have taken are false. There is no insurance against death.

Begin in your heart as the center and then start to expand your periphery. Imagine your physical boundaries dissolving as you become wider than your body. Then become even bigger than the room you are in, the house you are in. Keep expanding your boundaries; include all the people around you, your family, friends, all the people of your city and your country. Imagine your boundaries stretching beyond your country and including the whole world. Then become even wider and include other planets. You have a center, but no periphery. The whole cosmos becomes your periphery.

(Meditation taken from Vigyan Bhairav Tantra, Volume II by Osho, No.99)

As our awareness grows, we will begin to see that we are part of larger groups, and increasingly larger fields, and then we will inevitably see that 'others' are really also part of the same field. With more understanding, we move beyond the boundaries of the mind, which always tries to create walls and separation, and we begin to see that we are part of an ever-growing field that connects us all. The more we become aware of being part of something bigger, the more the sense of a separate 'I', the feeling of personal identity starts to dissolve.

Collective trauma

We have discussed the effects of personal trauma on our body and mind. Collective trauma refers to a traumatic event that did not happen to us directly, but to the social group, family or country, to which we belong. Some traumatic events that happened to former generations can continue to affect whole families. These can include the early death of children or of a parent, physical or psychological illnesses of family members, accidents, murder or other crimes, or when a former family member in some way has been made an outcast by the rest of his family. There are other traumas that affect whole societies. These include events like natural disasters, mass shootings, terrorism, famines or severe poverty, wars, pandemics, religious persecution and others.

Because of the bonding we feel to our family, religious or social group or country, we sometimes feel and behave as if such events have happened to us. A famine that happened two generations earlier might result in one wanting to hoard food or money now. Descendants of holocaust victims may feel resentment towards contemporary Germans.

The more we feel bonded to a social group, the more we feel connected to the trauma that this group had to suffer. Small children can become afraid without any immediate reason just because their mother is afraid. In a herd of animals, if one member of the herd sees a predator and starts to run all the other members of the herd will follow, even if they have not personally noticed the threat. Evolutionarily, this gives mammals a survival advantage over more primitive animals who do not create social bonds. Obviously 100 pairs of ears and eyes can see more than 2.

Under the influence of bonding, we may become scared just because some other member of our group is scared. If a father is depressed as a result of his wartime experiences, it may create depression in his child. The child might then behave as if the trauma that happened to his father happened to him personally and carry similar feelings that seem inexplicable to him. A parent who was abused as a child may have children who are afraid and anxious or even repeat his or her trauma themselves. And the most striking fact is that one does not understand why one feels or behaves this way.

Trauma experiences can travel over many generations depending on how severely the original event affected the family, and how successfully family members were able to process the activation the traumatic event created in them. In general, the traumatic activation tends to diminish over the generations, but it can still create a stress reaction some generations down. One may still feel the panic of one's grandfather who had to escape from a war zone to a foreign country and act out his fear by moving to a faraway place. It is as if the undigested past of our family members has to be digested by us. Their stress reaction travels to the next generation and we then try to fight or escape from an enemy who is no longer there.

Intergenerational trauma can affect whole societies. The children of genocide survivors sometimes exhibit symptoms of trauma without having been present during the original traumatic event. Studies show that issues such as risky health behaviours, anxiety and shame, food hoarding, overeating, authoritarian parenting styles, high emotional neediness, and low community trust are passed on from one generation to the next. The younger generation sometimes still lives in 'survival mode' even though in reality they are now living in safety and abundance.

What we consider to be 'karma' may be an undigested trauma repeating itself in later generations. Unconsciously, the condition of an earlier trauma is repeated in an attempt to find conscious resolution. The re-enactment that we described in Chapter One is now happening on a collective level. We unconsciously repeat the suffering of our ancestors in an attempt to resolve something that they needed to resolve, but could not.

Collective memory

Collective memory of trauma is different from individual memory because collective memory persists beyond the lives of the direct survivors of the events, and is remembered by group members who may be far removed from the traumatic events in time and space. These subsequent generations of trauma survivors, who never witnessed the actual events, may remember those events differently from the direct survivors. From generation to generation the construction of past events may take different shapes, and rather than leading to resolution may lead to the perpetuation of a trauma response.

This can sometimes be seen clearly in the victim/perpetrator dynamic that we work with in Family Constellation. The original victims may be more open to a perpetrator than their descendants, who have become stuck in an endless cycle of wanting revenge.

This collective memory of trauma is sometimes cultivated in certain families or cultures to create the sense of a collective self, a historical identity that provides a feeling of continuity between past, present and future. Unconsciously remembering a traumatic past and trying to find meaning in what happened promotes a vigilance to enhance group survival and restore a feeling of control.

In families of holocaust survivors, one often finds the strong determination that is passed on to later generations that one should never forget what happened. On the other side stands the blatant denial in some rightist groups that the holocaust ever happened. Real healing consists of two inner movements: The readiness to remember and the readiness to forget as well.

Examples from sessions

Indigenous people sometimes cling to the rituals and traditions of former generations and refuse to mix with others in order to keep their sense of identity. As a consequence, they sometimes suffer poverty, exploitation and injustice, just as their forefathers did.

A female client's grandmother at a very young age worked as a housemaid in some family and was chained there in order to prevent her from escaping home. This traumatic experience was re-enacted by the client, who had a six- or seven-year-old daughter, who was literally clinging to her legs during the group, not letting her move or even dance. She had never really liked her grandmother, but unconsciously she identified with her and created a situation with her own child to have a certain taste of how it must have felt for her grandmother to be unable to move freely and be chained like a slave. Her own child played a part in the re-enactment drama, representing the chain.

Chapter Five

Systemic Constellations

Systemic therapy understands the individual and his problems in the context of a larger group and the relationships within that group – particularly within his family system, which is the most important. In such a relational field, everyone's behaviour, feelings and attitudes have an effect on all the other family members. There are many systemic therapies and I will mostly refer here to the systemic approach called Family Constellation that was originally developed by Bert Hellinger, a German therapist. Over the years, there have evolved a variety of styles and methods of conducting a Family Constellation session, and during his lifetime Hellinger himself completely altered his way of doing these sessions according to various new discoveries he made.

In the original style, the client would choose representatives for certain family members from a group and place them in relation to each other, thus creating a kind of picture that revealed something about the relationship dynamics between the members of this family. In the latest approach, the representatives are not positioned according to the client's understanding and are not moved around by a facilitator, but rather are asked to observe their own inner impulses and follow them freely. What becomes manifest is a moving portrait of the family to which the client belongs, revealing the degree of intimacy, pain, love, or sense of abandonment that each one feels in relation to the others. It also exposes deep identifications and entanglements that result from the fact that everyone is bonded to a larger system, or collective, that includes many other people from both past and present. For example, in a constellation one can immediately see whom a representative is staring at, whom he is avoiding looking at, or if he is looking away as if missing someone. The moment a missing person is brought into the picture, a certain relief is felt.

Working in this way is not limited to a family. One can place members of any system in a constellation – members of a company, team, or class – and understand something of the relationship dynamics of that particular system.

Most events that lead to systemic entanglements are traumatic. The specialty of Family Constellation is that it shows how traumas of past generations and even of a whole country can leave their mark on the individual. While acknowledging the reality of trauma, Family Constellation offers no specific concept for healing it on a physiological level. Only the later approach to Family Constellation, where we work more with spontaneous movements of the representatives, is closer to the perspective of body-oriented trauma therapy, which considers trauma as an event that affects the body and its nervous system. This is because it usually unfolds in such a gradual and subtle way that it gives more time for integration.

In this chapter, I will discuss systemic traumas that happen in a relational field and how Family Constellation contributes to its understanding. In Chapter Seven, we will look at the therapeutic strategy when dealing with systemic trauma.

Central ideas and insights of Family Constellation

1. A systemic or Family Constellation reveals the presence of the collective energy field in which we live, which was described in the previous chapter. In other words, it brings to our awareness the collective unconscious mind. The closest and most obvious systemic field is the family we are born into. Within this field, anything that happens to one member has an influence on all other members. There are also bigger fields, like other social groups, religious groups and whole countries.

2. Everyone we are bonded to is part of this field, including people from former generations, whether dead or alive. Bonding happens either by birth or because of some common destiny or belief that binds a group together. A constellation immediately shows which representatives feel connected to each other or impact each other.

3. There are existential laws that govern how social systems function in general. These laws are not man made, but are principles of how the human mind works. They operate within our mind largely unconsciously and can be made visible through a Family Constellation.

4. The systemic field can be recreated by any group of people, who represent actual members of the system. These representatives can tap into the energy field of that system just by being appointed to a particular role, and without having been given any specific instructions. Their feelings, sensations

and movements reflect the impulses and feelings of those family members they represent. The emptier and more unprejudiced a representative is, the more accurately he is able to mirror the person he represents.

5. When asked to follow their spontaneous impulses, the representatives will reveal the relationship dynamics of the whole social or family system. They are sometimes called 'movements of the soul'. What happens in this collective field reflects at the same time what is happening in the collective unconscious mind of the individual.

6. The systemic laws that are extracted from observing these movements work on each member of the system equally. They bind the group together (law of belonging) and they create a hierarchical order within the group (law of order). When these laws are not respected, disturbance or disharmony is experienced by all the members of the system. Being in tune with these laws is experienced as relaxation, harmony and a feeling of flow.

7. There are movements that come from our personal unconscious mind and movements that arise from the collective unconscious mind and they are usually in conflict. In other words, what I personally desire, whether consciously or unconsciously, is often in conflict with what my family or collective group wants me to do.

8. The collective conscience is a powerful force that can only be transcended by respecting its intentions.

Family Constellations reveal these intentions and bring them to the awareness of the individual. With conscious awareness, a shift can happen from 'entangled' to 'healing' movements within a system, like when entangled strands of threads are sorted out. This is often accompanied by a shift from unconscious, bonding love to conscious and mature love.

9. All inner and outer movements arise from one existential life force and eventually lead back towards it. Everything is part of one universal system. When we are connected to these deeper existential life movements, we experience peace, harmony and healing. Then we are in tune with life as it is.

The three systemic laws

Now I will give a short summary of the basic systemic laws that I have described in detail in my book *The Roots of Love: A Guide to Family Constellation*. They are deduced from observing the interactions of the representatives in a constellation and are called 'the Law of Belonging', 'the Law of Order' and 'the Law of Balance'. They guide people's behaviour and way of thinking at an unconscious level and operate in all systems, whether a family or an organisation and are the way our mind structures the reality of how we relate to others. Consciously, because of personal desires and preferences, we often behave in ways that are in conflict with these laws and as a consequence we experience suffering. In other words, what we do consciously is often in conflict with our unconscious intentions and as our unconscious mind is really in charge of our lives, we will often do exactly the opposite of what we consciously think we want. For example, a person may say that he or she would like to have a successful relationship, but in reality, they do everything to sabotage this. In a constellation, it may become clear that this person is bonded with a parent or grandparent who lost their partner early, and therefore on a deep unconscious level they do not really want to have a more fulfilling life experience. Such unconscious bonds or identifications are at the root of most people's suffering.

The **Law of Belonging** relates to the fact that all members of a system have an equal right to be a part of that system and any exclusion or even judgment, which is a kind of exclusion, creates a disturbance in our collective conscience. Under that influence, family members, often from later generations, identify with those excluded or forgotten members of the system in an unconscious effort to include them. For example, the strange behaviour of a granddaughter might be the reflection of a schizophrenic grandmother who was never talked about inside the family. She may feel compelled to act in this way without really knowing why and without even having ever met her grandmother. Family destinies are full of such identifications, which may appear inexplicable at first, but become clear when one understands systemic laws.

Example from a session

A woman, whose father had been in a Nazi concentration camp and almost died there came to a session, because her son had joined a Neo-Nazi group and she was worried about it. She herself in her student years had been part of an anti-fascist left-wing group that was involved in sabotage acts against the government. It showed that she unconsciously carried the unexpressed rage of her father against fascists, while her son represented the side of the excluded ones, in this case the Nazis. Both represented the two sides, victim and perpetrator, of a traumatic experience in the life of her father.

To comprehend this, one needs to know about the strong bond that exists between victims and perpetrators and unless that bond is acknowledged and healed, someone from a later generation is compelled to pick up the thread and then continues to act out and play the role in an old drama.

The **Law of Order** relates to the hierarchy within a system, where each member has a certain place that belongs to them only. We have a deep sense about what is our rightful place within our family or within any system, and of our rights and boundaries, but often do not act accordingly. A child is a child and cannot behave like a parent and vice versa. A partner is an equal and neither the child nor the parent to the other.

We often do not behave in ways that respect ours or another's position and boundaries within the relational system, and as a consequence create a disturbance in our unconscious mind about what is our rightful place. Children may feel they are acting out of love for their mother when they start defending her against their father; they do not understand that they are interfering in the relationship between their parents and cannot see their own subtle arrogance in doing so. Or a person may become stuck with a feeling of hatred towards a parent, not understanding that this creates conflict and disturbance in his unconscious mind, which is profoundly aware of how much he owes his parents. As a consequence, such a person might unconsciously punish him or herself by failing to find success and fulfilment in life.

The **Law of Balance** relates to the fact that there is a deep inner sense of responsibility and fairness within our unconscious minds. Because of the bond we feel towards the members of our family, we may take over feelings of guilt and responsibility for the actions of others, even for someone of a former generation, which really does not belong to us. We may want to balance, compensate or take retributive actions for what others did or had to suffer. This also is a kind of interference in the lives of others, but is often done with a sense of righteousness or entitlement. Rather than flowing with the balancing movement of life, we want to take things into our own hands and as a consequence suffer, often quite unnecessarily.

I mentioned in Chapter Three about learning to distinguish between the guilt that is a result of our personal actions and that we have to carry and agree to, and another guilt that we take over for someone else out of a misguided sense of love.

These three laws operate simultaneously in all relational systems and impact strongly on our behaviour, our feelings and also our physical and mental health.

Systemic patterns of entanglement

An 'entanglement' describes the energetic involvement of one person in the life of another, usually a member of the family system including someone from a former generation. This identification happens most often with an excluded or forgotten member of the system and is an unconscious effort to maintain the memory of that person through repeating their life experience or suffering. It is as if one 'becomes' the other person and takes on his or her feelings, attitudes and behaviour.

When, for example, a boy identifies with his grandfather, who died when the mother was a young child, he may start to behave as if he is his mother's father, taking on a sense of importance and responsibility towards his mother, while at the same time carrying the feelings of his grandfather. It is not rare that children are given the names of the people that their parents have lost, and in this way a child is burdened from the very beginning and prevented from living his own life. Such children often remain bonded to their parents, unable to find their own purpose and joy in life.

In most families, we find multiple examples of such entanglements and identifications and it is often difficult to disentangle those knots and find out who is carrying whose feelings. When we are entangled, we forget who we really are, who the other really is, what period of time we live in, and what is our own responsibility and what is not. In psychological terms, we speak of projections, which are part of all relationships. We replay the dramas of the past; we shift feelings from one subject to another, from one object to another. If a woman is identified with her aunt who was in a concentration camp, she may look at her German husband with panic, behaving as if she is her aunt (shift in the subject) and treating her husband as if he is a perpetrator (shift in the object). This double shift is at the root of most relationship problems and creates an endless replay of the same drama, which really belonged to someone else.

By using representatives for each actual person, a constellation can make such identifications and entanglements obvious. When someone stands opposite the person with whom they are identified, they are forced to realise that they are not that person. In this way, the identification can be reduced or broken.

We have described how traumatic events activate our survival energy and how on the one hand this can increase our urge to bond while on the other impairing our ability to do so. The more traumatised a family or a social group is, the more closely the need to bond is felt, even by subsequent generations. And the closer the bonding, the more one becomes involved in the life of others and the more entanglements are created.

There are three basic patterns of entanglement that can be observed, all of which lead to suffering, and sometimes to illness and death.

In **'following'**, a person wants to stay close to another family member and experience what this person experienced. There is a refusal to let this person go. For example, when a child copies his mother's sadness or illness, his sense of belonging is strengthened. Or someone may want to follow a person who died by unconsciously creating an illness or refusing to fully take part in life.

In **'take over'** there is the desire to save a family member from suffering and take this suffering on oneself. The magical belief is that: If I myself suffer, the other will be relieved from this suffering'. It is as if one person could change another's destiny. Children who behave like heroes have such a tendency. As in all tragedies, the hero dies in the end without having achieved anything.

'**Atonement for guilt'** is a third way that leads to suffering. Rather than agreeing to a personal or family guilt and using it in a positive way, someone might want to die, or punish himself in an effort to create balance or payback for a crime.

Trauma fields

A constellation reveals the bonding patterns of a social group and how traumatic events can disturb bonding in general, and the interrelationships between the members of a family or social group. We will look at the different ways in which trauma can create dislocation in various relational fields and what effect this can have on the individual.

We live in many different relational fields at the same time, which mutually influence each other. Traumatic events can happen to an individual or to a whole group of individuals at one and the same time. They can influence a couple's relationship, a whole family or sometimes several generations of a family. They can happen to a bigger social group, like a religious or cultural group, or even to a whole country.

When, for example, a child dies, all the other family members will be affected, even those who are not yet born. The degree to which each family member has to bear the burden of the trauma may differ, but everyone will feel the effect of what happened. If the trauma happens to members of our religion or our country, this is also true, because we also bond to bigger social groups. The degree to which this affects individuals may differ, often depending on how close we were to those events or how close we feel to those who had to suffer it.

A constellation does not directly deal with shock trauma, but shock and systemic traumas are often interwoven. So, in order to fully heal a shock trauma, one may have to include dealing with the family system or other collective fields. If, for example, there has been a childhood accident and the relationship of the child to his or her parents is disturbed, it may be difficult to find a good resolution. This is an even bigger issue when dealing with incest or sexual abuse. Healing of all childhood traumas requires that the relationship of the child to his parents has to be included at some point.

Present family and relationship traumas

As described in the previous chapter, there is also bonding in couple relationships. According to the intensity of their bond, what happens to one partner will affect the other. If one partner dies, the other may want to follow him or her if there has been a strong bond between them. Or if one partner gets seriously ill the other becomes sick as well, in an unconscious attempt to save their partner from the disease.

A constellation can reveal such tendencies relatively quickly, just as it can show any disturbance in the relationship between two people. When we choose a representative for each person during a session, let them stand facing each other and then ask them to follow their impulses, we can discover certain information about the nature of their relationship. They may look at each other, or one of them may turn away or look at the floor. One representative might become fearful or angry or start crying. There are many possibilities that happen in the energy field between two people, and often a deeper truth about their relationship is revealed, which can be quite different from their previous understanding.

The most amazing fact is that the two representatives do not need to have any preliminary knowledge about the person they represent. It seems that when someone is without intention and is just receptive, they can access information that is part of an invisible energy field, quite similar to the way a radio can pick up electromagnetic waves from a distant station.

Relationship session example 1

In a session, the two representatives of a couple are not looking at each other; the woman looks at the floor, the man in another direction. The client, the woman in this case, gives some further information that there had been a miscarriage of their first child. After a representative of the dead child is placed on the floor, her representative starts to cry, the man turns around and is also moved to tears. Afterwards, they are both able to cry together about the loss of their child, the bond between them is healed and they can now embrace each other.

A traumatic event can affect the couple's relationship and can create a separation between them. If they are both able to come out of the initial shock and can process the feelings of their loss, the event can be healed and integrated. This in turn allows the relationship to continue and gain strength. If they both – or even only one of them – are/is unable to do that, the partners will start to grow apart.

The reason why a couple sometimes cannot digest a difficult event in their relationship or present family often has to do with traumatic and unprocessed events from their original families. But it is not always necessary to investigate the past.

Relationship session example 2

In a couple's session, the man starts to turn away from his wife, looking into the distance, while she starts to focus on him and become more and more desperate and upset because she is not getting any attention from him. The obvious conclusion is that the man is not available for his wife and she is showing a kind of dependency on him. The constellation indicates that there is someone in the original family of the man with whom he has an unresolved bond that does not allow him to look at his wife and be more present for her. There is also an unresolved issue in the wife's history, because she is overly focusing on the man, in fact she is starting to behave like a small child seeking attention from a parent.

On gathering information about the original family of each partner, we learn that the man was separated from his mother early in life. As his parents separated, he stayed with the father and had almost no contact with his mother. That explains why he is looking away: He is searching for his mother. Being separated from her remained an unresolved trauma in his mind and during his adult life he kept repeating a pattern of expecting women to be his substitute mother. If a woman did not show unconditional love for him, he had a tendency to leave and look for someone else.

The wife, on the other hand, had a father who had been to war and after his return was depressed and emotionally unavailable to his family. This left her mother deeply unsatisfied and she was unable to find any other personal fulfilment in her life. The session shows how she projected her unfulfilled need to be seen by her father onto her partner, at the same time copying her mother's inability to find her own fulfilment when a partner was not available. Also, her tendency to 'mother' the other was taken over from her own mother and was an attempt to get attention through giving love.

In a relationship, both parties are responsible for any conflict between them and this can rarely be resolved unless the unresolved issues and traumas from the past, usually from their family of origin, are addressed. If this is not dealt with, the same conflicts keep endlessly repeating themselves and there is no resolution, because the cause is not in the present, but in a past trauma. They need each other to re-enact the original trauma, so they can neither separate nor fully resolve the conflict. A mutual dependency is created, where neither of them is available to the other as an adult partner. What each of them is actually doing is living out a childhood trauma, trying to get the attention and love that they missed as a child from their parent.

To successfully heal bonding issues with one's parents, one first needs to acknowledge the feelings of disappointment, anger and pain about not having been fully seen as a child. Secondly, one needs to find a way to accept the fact that one's parents had their own unresolved traumas and therefore what has been received from them was all that was possible. Only then does one become capable of letting go of the attachment to the parents and giving up the hope of finally getting more. Then one can move beyond childhood bonding and become an adult.

As these examples show, there are traumatic events that happen to a couple directly, as in a miscarriage for example, or if one partner dies suddenly. And there are also traumatic events that happened in the original families of each partner as we saw in our last example.

Traumas in the original family

Traumatic events in our original family can affect every aspect of our adult life. It can often be a mixture of interwoven events. For example, a child may not be able to deal with a traumatic accident or medical procedure if his parents are not able to support him in an appropriate way. And if they have not been able to process the traumas from their own childhood, they are not able to do this, which leads to a secondary traumatisation of their child. The unprocessed shock trauma of the child can then lead to developmental deficits.

It is sometimes difficult for a therapist or someone in the helping professions to know where to even begin the healing process. When we consider events from past generations as well, then it sometimes seems unbelievable how many traumatic events families and children had to endure.

Here some examples:

A single mother of 45 years of age is unable to handle her teenage son, who frequently has violent outbursts.

She has been avoiding any confrontation with her ex-husband or son for many years and things are getting more and more out of control. Her fear of conflict is related to her experience in childhood. When she was 6 years-old she lost one of her eyes in an accident. While playing with her doll she had accidentally stabbed herself in the eye with a knife, eventually losing the eye. She had to spend many months in hospital and remembered lying alone in her bed immobile and frozen, with only her doll for company.

Upon investigating her parents, she spoke about her fear of her mother who used to have frequent violent outbursts. She was the first-born child and her younger brother, her mother's second child, had died at the age of three when this client had just turned five. All her life she had felt that something was basically wrong with her, and only after starting therapy at the age of 35 did she feel for the first time that this may not be true.

In this sample, it is clear that in order to heal the shock of losing an eye, in combination with a long hospital stay and several medical operations – which is already a multiple trauma for a young child – it was also essential to heal the relationship with her mother. It is likely that her accident and the stabbing of her eye arose from an unconscious self-rejection, in an attempt to follow her dead brother. It was also a way of finally gaining her parents' attention, which she lost after the death of her brother. After her accident, her parents were overwhelmed by guilt. Eventually, the past history of her mother might also need to be examined in order to understand why she could not get over the death of her son and reacted with violence towards her daughter.

In another constellation, a mother (the client) turns away from her husband and children. It turns out that she is identified with her grandmother, who lost her own father very early in life. As an adult, she had then married a much older man, a kind of father figure for her, who was already married with 4 children and 'only' symbolically married the grandmother. After his death, she had to take care of these stepchildren. The client felt sorry for her grandmother and wanted to alleviate her pain and in this way behaved towards her children as if they were not her own, copying the grandmother, who had to take care of someone else's children, which she resented. As a consequence, she ignored her own children, who started to get more and more upset with their mother.

In a constellation, we can see our unconscious identifications with members of our family system very clearly. When we stand in front of someone we are identified with or unconsciously bonded to, we begin to feel this bonding love, which is already a great relief. Our tears may flow and we might start for the first time to experience how deeply we are connected to someone from our family past. Unless this love is felt and deeply experienced, no real transformation can take place. Any intellectual knowledge about unconscious identifications will not suffice. Only after this bonding love is felt and acknowledged, can one grow beyond it and love can enter a new dimension, where we recognise that we each have our own life destiny. Mature love is capable of respecting that.

Larger trauma fields

As described, one unique contribution of Family Constellation is to demonstrate how we are not only bonded to family members we know, but also to those of previous generations we have never met. That means that all the multiple traumas of previous generations also influence and mould our life in the present.

It has been scientifically shown through a new field of science called epigenetics that traumatic life events or environmental circumstances many generations back can alter the way our genes work. They do not alter the DNA sequence of our body cells, but they alter the way our body reads a DNA sequence. That means certain parts of our DNA may get switched on or off. It has been found that, for example, a past period of starvation in one generation can leave a chemical mark on certain genes of a person's DNA that then can get passed on to future generations. This can explain how the traumas of our ancestors still alter our way of behaving and responding to certain life situations, even though we have never been exposed ourselves to the same or even similar events.

A less scientific and more psychological explanation is to assume the existence of an energy field that can span many generations, and that binds its members together. It is a known fact that mothers know when their child is in danger even if she is in a faraway continent. It has also been shown that when primates on a remote island learn a certain skill, other primates in faraway locations learn the same skill at approximately the same time without the possibility of any contact between them. In other words, not only learning, but also traumas affect those who are part of the same energy field.

We all have experienced the impact it can have when we enter a room with a number of depressed, frightened or angry people in it, and how differently we are influenced when the people in that room are joyful and happy. Every family, every social group and every country creates these energy fields around them, and the influence this can have on the individual, especially if they are exposed to it for a long time, can be very powerful. Such collective energy fields are sometimes not easy to detect and they can make us blind and prejudiced towards the reality outside of it.

I personally remember when I first left Germany to spend a long period abroad, what a relief it felt for me to leave my 'fatherland' behind. It gave me the feeling that now I could finally breathe, and a sense of freedom entered my body and mind. Upon my return, after several months I could sense myself re-entering a very familiar energy cloud. It is like a fish in the sea, which does not become aware of the water he is in until he is thrown out of it.

Every social group creates a collective field around itself, and in order to create some awareness and clarity about this field it is essential to move out of it, at least temporarily. We easily become adapted to the social energy field we live in, and we can become part of a very limited and prejudiced worldview without even noticing. This has happened in the past in almost all religions, countries, and cultures. Identification always leads to blindness, not only if it is an identification with a person, but even more so if we identify with the beliefs and attitudes that are those of a country, culture or religion. The family field is small and we sometimes see that other families are different, but if a person lives his whole life in one country or remains part of one religion, they may never notice that they have been wearing coloured glasses.

Personally, I was quite lucky to meet my spiritual master Osho early in my life, which saved me from becoming a 'good' member of society, a fate that happens to many after the rebellious student years are over. Without the support of an enlightened being, it is not easy to remain in an outsider position for long, trying to keep a state of mind that is less under the influence of the collective conscience.

Under Osho's guidance we have been running large international therapy courses, where participants sometimes come from more than 20 different countries, with different cultural, religious and social backgrounds. In such situations, it becomes much easier for each individual person to look outside his or her own coloured glasses of social, cultural, religious and family conditioning. Learning from others how life can be looked at from so many standpoints and perspectives one realises, maybe for the first time, how much one has been living in a tiny box of limiting beliefs and ideas.

It may not always be so obvious that we ourselves come from a trauma field, whether it includes only our family or a much larger group. But after many years of working with social systems and trans-generational trauma I am a lot more aware that traumas can be found in every family and every country, and that the past traumas of former generations still have a profound effect on our lives. The conditioning following traumatic events, the collective memory and stories around it can sink deeply into the sub-conscious layers of our mind. If the Nazis had tortured our grandfather, we may have a subtle feeling of discomfort when visiting Germany even now. If a former family member was part of a separatist terrorist group, it may be easier for the child of a later generation to be ready to die than to talk about it openly. We hold secrets for our families; we defend our country and take over guilt and pay the debts for those who are part of our religion or culture, even if they are long dead. We are living out the past traumas of our ancestors without realising it; we are re-enacting what they could not resolve in their lives. The trauma field of our family and of our country surrounds us from the moment we are born and it is not easy even to notice that we are under the influence of collective bonding.

Example from a session

A Bulgarian man in a group session reports that his 4-year-old daughter suffers from epilepsy, which developed after he divorced his wife. The background information about his and his ex-wife's original families is that she comes from a communist family with a famous communist leader, while he comes from an anti-communist family. His grandfather was sentenced to death by the communist rulers at that time, which was not carried out, but the grandfather was forced to live outside the city away from his family.

The constellation showed that his representative looked straight into the distance away from his child and ex-wife. The representative for his wife looked at the floor and the daughter stood alone, nobody looking at her and she also looked into the distance, just like the representative for her father.

Understanding family dynamics, we know that a person who has been excluded from the whole system is always represented again in a later generation. So, the guiding question for a facilitator usually is, who could have been excluded here or who is missing? We also know that it is not only family members who belong to the system, but also those who become bonded to the family through a particular destiny or traumatic event. The traumatic event of the past here could be the communist rule, the violence, life threat or sometimes murder that people suffered during their dictatorship.

So, our working hypothesis is that the woman remembers the victims of the communists and looks at them on the floor, because they were obviously disliked and persecuted by members of her original family. He, on the other hand, remembers the communists, who were hated in his family and are therefore remembered by him. This would also explain why they married each other, an unconscious and failed attempt to heal the bonds of the past. Hatred always reveals a very strong bond.

I choose representatives for the missing people, letting a few victims lie down in front of the ex-wife and a few perpetrators stand in front of the man. If a hypothesis is correct, it creates movements in the constellation and has an effect on everyone. Now the representatives are invited to follow their spontaneous impulses.

As the constellation continued, it showed not only how a couple who had never experienced the time of communist dictatorship themselves still carried the energy of what happened in the previous generation into their lives and into their relationship, but also how even their child suffered the consequences. The constellation finally also revealed that it was actually the man who had the epileptic impulse (his representative during the constellation almost had an epileptic fit) and his daughter took it over for her father to save him from it.

Without going into all the details of the constellation, I want to mention that healing happened when representatives for communists and anti-communists could finally look into each other's eyes, facing the wounds they inflicted upon each other. And when we finally also brought a representative for the country the representative for the child could not stop crying. She showed the greatest love and felt the pain of the whole country.

Part II: Healing Trauma

In part 1, I have outlined the somatic and systemic approach about how to understand trauma. While a somatic approach primarily deals with the frozenness of our physiology, a systemic approach investigates how trauma affects the relationships between the members of a relational field. In a traumatised system, where healthy attachment is disrupted, a constellation will show that the movements of the representatives become frozen or fixated. In a healthy relationship system, where love flows easily, there is a constant movement of coming closer or moving apart. In the case of trauma, these movements towards others or away from others tend to stop.

Trauma healing can be approached from different angles. In a primarily somatic approach, we start with the body and try to facilitate a discharge of the frozen life energy. It is less relevant to know what caused a trauma state in the first place and psychological issues may only be dealt with to the degree that they promote a healthy physiological self-regulation. However, if psychological causes are not also addressed at some point, the danger is that a person may unconsciously repeat an event over and over again. For example, if we only process the physiological charge caused by an accident without also looking at a possible psychological cause that led to the accident (providing that there is such a cause), we may continue to have similar accidents.

In a more psychological approach, including Family Constellation, it will often be best to first investigate what could possibly cause a traumatic state, what unresolved traumas in the family past there are, and what hidden systemic entanglements are at the root of a problem. If there is a history of trauma in a family, it is often not so easy to determine where to begin, what are relevant facts and what are not. Family Constellation or systemic constellations deal with collective or systemic traumas that happen in a systemic relational field, not with shock trauma.

Unless a therapist knows how to include the body in his approach and at the same time can address psychological issues, healing may be incomplete. Healing always means that something from the past has been completed. This includes both a psychological completion as well as a somatic completion. In this book, my attempt is to show how these can come together.

Realms of trauma

A traumatic event can happen in different areas of life. Even though these areas may overlap, it is good for a therapist to be able to distinguish between them and be clear about what he is dealing with. Here is a short review, some of it we already mentioned in earlier chapters:

Trauma can happen in one's personal life, either in adulthood or in childhood. It can be a one-time event (shock trauma) or a series of smaller events that have an accumulative effect. When this happens in childhood, it can severely disturb healthy childhood development (developmental trauma). There are many categories of trauma depending on what caused the trauma reaction and they all need a slightly different approach, but it is beyond the scope of this book to discuss this. Our focus here is more on traumas that happen in a relational field and that affect our bonding. In the relational field of a family, the traumatic event may not have happened to the person directly, but to another family member or the family as a whole. This can be the present family (which means the event took place in adulthood) or in the family of origin (which means it happened in childhood). Because of the bonding we have towards our family members, it affects us as well. This is called secondary traumatisation.

There are also other traumas that we did not witness directly, but which happened before our lifetime or in a previous generation, sometimes even a few generations earlier. This is called trans-generational trauma. How many generations are affected by a traumatic event usually depends on how severe and devastating the event was and how resilient those people who had to suffer it were. Trans-generational trauma can relate only to a specific family or to a bigger social group, like an entire religious or cultural group, or a nation as a whole. As we are also bonded to these larger units, we are also affected by traumatic events that happen, for example, in our country.

Additionally, I also want to mention past life traumas that happened in an earlier incarnation. Whether a trauma state relates to an event from a past life or a past generation is often not easy to determine, but when we take a more pragmatic therapeutic approach, where we focus more on what is helpful for a client, then this may not even matter that much.

We can see here that there are multiple possibilities of how trauma can affect our lives and we often have several different traumas to deal with at the same time. Therefore, neither a purely somatic, nor a purely systemic approach may be sufficient for trauma healing. In this section, I will also discuss how integration could be achieved in one's therapeutic work.

Chapter Six

A Somatic Approach to Healing Trauma

In this chapter, I will summarise a few important principles of a somatic approach to healing trauma. The central point is how to help the body to discharge, digest and integrate the severed survival energy that was activated after having been confronted with a life-threatening event. This unprocessed energy that is trapped in the body's physiology is responsible for creating symptoms of post-traumatic stress and prevents a full and more whole life experience in the present. As by definition, trauma is an overwhelming event; the therapeutic approach is about avoiding the experience of being overwhelmed.

Body and mind need to be understood as one organic unit that operate together and mutually influence each other. Somatic approaches to therapy usually start by working with the body intending to reach to the level of the mind, while psychological approaches start with the mind intending to affect the physiology. To understand how our intellectual mind and physiology are linked together, it is helpful to have some basic understanding about the way our brain is structured.

The triune brain

The triune brain is a model of our brain as consisting of three structures that are added on top of one another during evolution, and are viewed as somehow independently conscious. This model was proposed by neuroscientist Paul MacLean in 1960 and propounded in 1990 and even though it is very simplified and no longer considered to be an up-to-date model, it still helps one to understand the complexity of brain functioning. The model basically explains that there are three parts of the brain that can work separately while at the same time working as one unit.

The oldest is called the brainstem or reptilian brain, as this is shared with all reptiles. It is responsible for all instinctive functions and behaviours, like fight and flight and also feeding. When our core need of survival and safety is challenged, this part of the brain is in charge.

The next is the limbic system or paleo-mammalian brain, which developed later and is home to functions like emotion, motivation and bonding behaviour. It developed in animals as they started to bond with each other and is involved when the issue is about satisfying our needs, which is a dopamine dominated behaviour, the wish to feel good.

The latest development is the neo-cortex or neo-mammalian brain that developed more or less exclusively in primates and is home to all intellectual and higher brain functions, like language, thinking, explicit memory, planning and making more complex and deeper social connections.

In reference to this model, one could divide human experience into sensing (body), feeling (heart) and thinking (mind/neo-cortex). This also relates to our core needs of safety, satisfaction and connection.

Sensing the body

We have discussed in Chapter One how our body is affected by trauma. Trauma happens after events where our sense of safety is challenged. We have to respond fast and there is no time for other regulating mechanisms of the brain to come in. Thinking and feeling take time, but in moments of danger our reaction has to be fast in order to secure survival. So, the brainstem takes control and we react instinctively and indiscriminately, as a reflex, without thinking about what we are doing. It can be observed that in moments of intense danger humans respond to a situation just like primitive animals. Therefore, the key to healing trauma is to reach the level of the brainstem, where basic survival responses originate. And the language of the brainstem is sensing, not thinking and not even feeling.

Connecting to our body is not always easy, nor necessarily a pleasant experience. We tend to forget our body and remember it only when it hurts or does not function in the way we expect. Learning to listen to our body and respect its messages is one of the key elements in healing trauma.

Tracking our physical sensations or more precisely our 'felt sense', is a fundamental skill to be learned when trying to heal from trauma. Psychologist Eugene Gendlin has coined the term and he describes it like this: "A felt sense is not a mental experience but a physical one. *Physical*. A bodily awareness of a situation or person or event. An internal aura that encompasses everything you feel and know about the given subject at a given time."[2] (Focusing-oriented psychotherapy)

All our life experiences are accompanied by physical sensations and can be more accurately described through the felt sense that blends together all the information that we receive, both from our external

---

[2] Gendlin, Eugene (1982): *Focusing*

senses and our body's internal awareness. Emotions and thoughts can contribute or change our felt sense, yet the felt sense is not a thought or an emotion. It is something we feel through being in a living body; it may be vague or sometimes complex and is constantly changing. It usually is experienced either as pleasant or unpleasant.

Most of the time, we do not pay much conscious attention to physical sensations and if I were to ask you what you feel if I take your hand and hold it, you might say that you notice my hand holding your hand. But this is only a supposition; it is a thought, not a feeling. Then you might say that you feel that I care, but also this is only a thought, an idea. What you really feel would be the warmth or the pressure of my hand; only this sensation is real, all else is just a mental conclusion. The sensations we receive from our body at each moment are usually ignored unless there is severe physical pain or discomfort.

Different from emotions and thoughts, sensations can be located in a specific place in our body. The awareness of sensations connects us to our body and this is not only the basis for all healing, but also the foundation for all inner development and growth. The body is our base; through the body we are grounded in reality.

To be more accurate, it is not a chair that makes us feel comfortable, but the sensations that come when we sit in it. Similarly, it is never really another person who causes an emotion in us, but seeing or hearing that person triggers physical reactions in our body and when these signals reach the brain they are translated into a certain emotional state. Our body responds from a past memory without our even being aware of it and a present stimulus can trigger an automatic response that may cause our heart rate to go up or create other changes in our physiology that we eventually interpret as being angry or sad or happy.

So, it can be really helpful to ask, while being anxious or sad or angry: what is actually going on in the body that tells me that I am feeling this way? Where in my body do I feel it and what exactly is the sensation that accompanies my feeling? In a therapeutic session, I will often ask a client, who might vaguely say: "I am okay" or "I am anxious", to describe more accurately what physical sensations give him that sense. He might then say that he is feeling a tingling or trembling in the chest or butterflies in the stomach. Every sensation has a location, maybe a size or shape and a specific physical quality that can be described in words like cold, hot, constricted, tingling, streaming, dense, heavy, electric, numb, vibrating or other similar words. By asking a person to specify the physical experience that accompanies his feeling or thought, he will learn how to be more in contact with his body and more grounded in the physical realm of his existence.

Exercise

Sit comfortably, maybe with eyes closed, and notice the different sensations that come to you from different parts of your body, moment after moment. Try to feel them more deeply, rather than thinking about them. Notice that there are pleasant sensations and unpleasant ones and also become aware of how your attention shifts from one sensation to another in a constant stream.

How would you best describe each of these sensations? Find some words or phrases that would best describe what you are sensing in each moment, maybe even using metaphors. For example, you might say, "My feet are cold and frozen as if they are in ice cold water", or it might be more like a shivering. Or "There is some pounding pain in my right knee", or "I have some tingling sensations in my fingers as if there is an electric current", or "My belly feels warm and full, like after a good meal" and so on. You can either write these words down or report them to a partner if you can find a way to do this exercise with someone else.

You might notice that sometimes your attention gets stuck on the same sensation and your mind becomes focused on it. This is not a problem, and after a while you could ask yourself: Is there anything else that I am aware of happening in my body?

Help your attention to move on and become aware of all the different sensations that are happening at each moment.

This exercise may seem boring in the beginning and not very exciting, but it can help us to be more connected to our body so we become grounded in the reality of the present moment. Unlike our thoughts, our body is always in the Here and Now.

The 3 phases of trauma healing

By learning to sense our body and be more in the present, we have already learnt one important step towards healing trauma. I have explained in my book on counselling (The Zen Way of Counseling, O-Books, 2009), how a session can be divided into three phases – which I have described as support, confrontation and integration. When we apply this to trauma therapy, the first phase would be about building a sense of safety and trust, something that was lost during a traumatic event. All of a sudden, the world no longer felt like a safe place, the ground was swept away from under our feet and we lost the feeling of trust and being grounded. Sometimes it happens that even our own body no longer feels like a safe place, which is the reason traumatised people often become dissociated from their bodies. Depending on how disturbing the traumatic event was, and how resilient a person is, it can take quite some time to come back to the body and regain a sense of relative safety. Unless this happens, at least to some extent, a session cannot proceed.

In the second phase, we slowly and gradually start to deal with the traumatic event, which is a kind of confrontation, because now we have to begin to face whatever was so disturbing, overwhelming, frightening. Healing is a process of digesting and integrating an experience and one needs to find the right pace at which this can happen without overwhelming our system. To sound this out, according to the potential of the client, is the challenge in trauma therapy. One has to be willing to give up the wish to experience only good feelings, while at the same time learning to see and respect one's limits and not challenge oneself too far. Often therapists and clients alike confuse feeling safe with feeling good. When we feel safe enough, we become capable of facing that which is unpleasant and uncomfortable. This implies dealing with feelings of panic, anger despair and pain and an experience that shook us to the roots.

In the third phase, we enter a process of giving our body and mind the necessary time to slowly, step by step, integrate the unlocked survival energy that is emerging from its frozen state. The whole body has to reorganise itself, sometimes after years of being stuck in a locked state, and we have to become accustomed to a new strength and aliveness. As one gains more trust and strength, it becomes possible to access even deeper, still unprocessed elements of the traumatic event and in this way slowly, layer by layer, one's life energy can be reclaimed. Only after a certain integration has been achieved can other aspects of a traumatic experience be dealt with.

Obviously, the distinction between these three phases is theoretical, as in practice there is often no such clear separation between them. In a session, there is a natural flow between giving support, confronting a person with a challenge and taking time for integration. One will switch many times between going further and retreating, depending on a client's capacity to handle activated states. The aim is to avoid repeating the experience of being overwhelmed, while staying in touch with a basic sense of relative safety and supporting the body to find its innate way of self-regulation.

Safety and grounding

At the beginning of a session or any other exploration of one's inner world, it is helpful to use some time to examine whether one is in touch with a sense of safety. This can be directly related to outer circumstances or can be only an internal feeling.

The more we have an inner sense of feeling safe, the less we need to control our environment. And the more this inner sense is missing the more we try to be in control of the outside. Both disturbed childhood development and traumatic experiences can shatter this inner sense of being safe, and then the work in therapy is to help to rebuild it. And this starts with creating a safe environment on the outside to give a person the feeling of being in control of his life, needs, decisions, feelings and body. Ultimately, the aim is to experience one's own body as a safe container for all life experiences.

In reality, safety as such is always relative, because existentially there is no absolute safety. Life is intrinsically unsafe in the sense that anything can happen any moment and the future always remains uncertain and unknown. Therefore, the need to control our life is ultimately bound to fail. So, the learning is to feel safe with the uncertainties of life. Developing such trust starts in childhood when we first learn to be in control of our body, our needs and – to a certain degree – of our environment. Children learn this when they explore saying 'no' to someone, or to something that they do not like or want. By first learning control, they later become capable of trust and eventually letting go of personal desires.

Trauma creates a wound in us because an event overwhelmed us suddenly and unexpectedly and we completely lost the sense of having any control. Therefore, the work in trauma therapy is to first re-establish this sense, which will repair our ability to trust and let go.

Creating a safe environment can start in a simple way by exploring where in the room the client would like to sit, maybe in relation to the door or a window, what the right distance from the therapist is, whether he is sitting comfortably or maybe needs an extra pillow. It is also important that for the duration of the session there should be no disturbance from outside: phones should be turned off and noise from outside should be kept at a minimum. This and other simple arrangements will help the client to feel safe and that he is being taken care of.

Addressing the client's inner sense of safety and how much he is in contact with it, or not, is subtle and needs to be constantly checked throughout the session. As this sense is damaged in trauma, it is important to keep investigating what a person, in a certain moment of his present life, would need in order to feel safe. Even if a client cannot say what would make him feel safe, asking about it changes the focus of his mind from the trauma to a resource, which in turn can have the effect of releasing some of his high activation or tension and thus facilitate a more grounded feeling of safety.

In general, it is helpful when working with trauma to give a client the sense of being in control of his own process, for example by reassuring him that the session will only proceed if he is ready and gives his okay. As explained previously, in trauma the body was overwhelmed by an event and is still struggling to gain back the lost control. Peter Levine calls post-traumatic stress (PTS) "an abnormal prolongation of what had originally been a normal response to a severely threatening situation. PTS symptoms are incomplete responses that have become frozen in time." Helping the body to realise that an event is over is one of the main goals of trauma therapy.

Establishing a contact with the ground we are standing on also contributes to creating a sense of safety. **Grounding** means allowing the gravitational forces to flow through us and connect with the center of gravity in our belly, which is also called the hara center. This helps us to come in contact with a certain trust, a feeling of security that arises when we feel that we are part of this earth and not separate from it.

Centering means to turn our attention inside to a point where the identification with anything outside is diminished or disappears. Ultimately, it is the awareness of our inner center, which is empty with no sense of an 'I'. Therefore, it is not really accurate to say that 'I am centered'. In the East, especially in Japan in the Zen tradition, it is a common practice and learning not to act from will or desire, but from one's inner emptiness. A Zen archer, for example, allows the gravitational pull to fill the hara center and eventually a moment comes when he is filled, and the arrow shoots by itself. He certainly takes aim, but the gravitational force takes the arrow to the target.

Grounding, centering and feeling safe are all interlinked and mutually support each other. In fear and insecurity, we tend to lift up and become ungrounded, while a sense of safety makes us more centered and grounded. Conversely, when we are more connected to the ground beneath our feet, a feeling of safety slowly returns. There are many grounding and centering exercises that can be helpful when dealing with an overwhelming experience and this is just one of them:

Exercise

Come into a standing position, placing your legs shoulder width apart. Bend your knees slightly and allow your whole body to be relaxed and your mouth slightly open. Close your eyes for a moment and imagine you are like a tree whose roots go deep into the ground. Imagine that they come out of the soles of your feet and reach to the center of the earth. Allow your breathing to flow normally.

After a while imagine a slight breeze moving your body backwards and forwards and from side to side in different, irregular directions. Your feet should remain firmly on the ground as if they are part of the earth. Allow your knees and your whole body to be flexible, just like a tree as it bends and sways with the wind. You can start with very small movements and gradually allow them to become bigger; whatever feels easy and comfortable for you.

In your own time you can end the movement, as if the wind has finally stopped. Remain standing still with your knees still slightly bent. Now feel the center of gravity in your lower belly. You can place your hands there if you want. Take another moment to sense that before you come back.

Healthy boundaries

In trauma, we lose connection to ourselves, to our body and sometimes also to the awareness of the boundary between ourselves and others, or between ourselves and our environment. Our skin defines our physical boundary and beyond that there is an energy field around the body, which is called the aura.

Through sensing the aura, we know if someone is coming too close or if we are too close to someone else. The aura also has a certain form, shape and extension that can be ruptured or deformed by a traumatic event. As a result, it can become difficult for us to address or even feel when another person is trespassing and invading our physical space or privacy. Or, conversely, it may be difficult to sense when we invade someone else's physical space.

Any abuse, whether physical, sexual or emotional is a boundary invasion. When children grow up in an environment where physical, emotional and mental boundaries are not respected, they become confused and insecure about their own and other people's boundaries. In extreme cases it can lead to losing their sense of personal identity.

Boundary transgressions are very common in families. In the beginning, children do not yet have a sense of boundaries and only slowly develop the sense that their own needs and preferences are different to those of their caretakers. Parents can either support this process or be an obstacle as their child tries to develop healthy boundaries, depending on whether they were able to learn this themselves. They may be either invasive and not allow the child to have his own private space, or they be unavailable when the child needs to bond and get support.

Boundaries are defined and established through learning to say 'no'. If we did not learn this in childhood or were not supported in doing so, this will affect our sense of personal identity and how safe we feel within ourselves. In a session, a client can be supported to learn and establish his boundaries by inviting him to be more in charge of his own process and giving him permission to say 'no' or 'stop' at any time. The therapist himself needs to be clear and clean about his boundaries and neither invade the space of the client, nor allow the client to invade his space. This starts with a simple awareness about proper physical distancing and goes so far as not starting a personal relationship with a client, or being available 24 hours a day. We will come back to this topic in Chapter Twelve.

Example from a session

I worked with a female client who had been abused to re-establish her fight response. After feeling resourced, she started to have sensations in her arms and we explored them and after a while I suggested that she stretch both arms away from herself as if pushing someone away, feeling how far she wanted someone to be away from her in order to feel safe. This felt empowering to her and we explored this further by inviting her to also use sentences like, "You cannot come closer than this", or to simply say "No". In this way, she could reconnect with a sense of power and control over her life and re-establish her sense of physical and emotional boundaries.

Personal physical boundaries can also be strengthened and defined through touch, including self-touch. Self-touch is safer, as in the case of abuse, touching a client, even only slightly and respectfully, can be associated with the original boundary violation and then can be experienced as invasive rather than supportive. But touch also has the potential to strengthen a person's sense of his body as a physical 'container' that contains all sensations and feelings. The more we can sense this container and know its capacity, the more we become capable of handling strong life experiences. For example, a person could touch his skin and certain body parts and say aloud: "This is my body/my arm/my leg". In this simple way, he could learn to regain a lost sense of where the physical body begins and ends.

As we will see, Family Constellation is a simple and effective method of bringing clarity into boundary violations within relationship systems and can contribute to establishing healthy boundaries between others by finding the right position within the system. It further clarifies emotional boundaries by showing whose feelings we are carrying and whose needs we are expressing.

Building resources

Resourcing is a method where the client is brought into contact with anything that helps him maintain a sense of self and inner integrity. There can be outer resources, such as individuals, special places or objects and inner resources, such as personal qualities and abilities. Resources can be experienced on a physical, emotional, psychological, social and spiritual level. They are unique to the individual and can also change during a session, but they always help and strengthen the client in the face of difficulties or disruption, which otherwise would lead to **retraumatisation**.

Coming into contact with a resource usually allows a discharge of the held activation and is therefore experienced as a relief. If the release does not happen, it is generally an indication that a resource has not been found and one needs to search for something else.

Resources can change over time and according to the situation. After a traumatic event, we can easily lose touch with our resources and sometimes help is needed to find them again. Our bodily reactions are the measuring stick to determine whether we are in contact with a resource or not.

In my experience, my biggest resource was love – the love that I felt for my wife, the love I knew she had for me and the love that poured over me from so many people from around the world. Not only that, but one of my friends travelled all the way from Europe to be with me and support me for the remaining 2-3 days before leaving South Africa, but also other friends who were always available to talk to me on the phone.

Another important resource was my training in meditation and what I learned over so many years of sitting in the presence of an enlightened master. That kept me sane. When my mind was torturing me, endlessly asking questions such as 'Why did I not do this or that?' and 'What if ....', and my heart wanted to burst, I just sat down, closed my eyes and let the inner craziness be there without doing anything at all.

There were some other people who helped me in different ways. There was the other diver on the boat, who was, together with me, trying his best to bring Meera back and whom I never saw again, but will never forget. There was this one lady from the staff, who came running over the day after and hugged me and cried with me. There was the manager of the resort, the undertaker, someone from the embassy and Meera's brother in Japan, who all helped me with many practical details to sort out, legal papers and doing all kinds of things that are needed in such a situation, and which are the very last things anyone would want to do in such a moment.

And I should not forget that having some money in my hand and a car was also an important resource and help in that moment, as well as my own ability to find my way and orientation in a foreign country. I want to mention another resource here, especially as nowadays there is so much complaint about social media: It was extremely helpful to have the opportunity to connect and receive support through social media channels and the internet.

The word 'resource' may sound a bit technical. It basically means anything in a given situation that helps us to cope with it. Naturally, one of our biggest resources as human beings is love and our ability to make connections with one another. To lose that capacity is one of the biggest challenges and tragedies that sometimes happens to people, who have suffered from trauma.

There are outer resources, like a special place in nature or one's personal space, or maybe a special object. Also, money can be a resource, and realising that one has enough time. And, of course, certain people can be our resource – friends, lovers, family members, teachers, and therapists. Sometimes the same person can be both a resource and a trigger for stress. For example, parents are usually both; for a child they are his support and at the same time often part of his trauma. In that case, it can be helpful and strengthening to remember only in what way they were a resource and for the moment to blank out any other considerations.

Besides such outer resources, there are also inner resources, like a personal skill, ability or talent.

Exercise

Take a piece of paper and make a list of the resources that are available to you in your life now, and those that you had when you were young. Specify outer and inner resources.

The building of resources is an important part of trauma work, especially because in trauma a person often loses contact with his resources. Rediscovering resources prepares the client to face challenges without getting overwhelmed by them. Coming in touch with a resource usually facilitates the discharge of an activated trauma state.

Example of a resource-oriented approach to a session

A client, whose child had developed a tumour in his legs, became very activated when talking about it. Without entering this issue further, we started by first helping her to find a resource in her body, a place in her body where she could rest and have a sense of well-being. Then I asked her if there was anything at all that was a slight relief for her in dealing with the situation. She mentioned that the doctors said that it was not a life-threatening illness. Her body immediately discharged by breathing out deeply.

Next she mentioned about the latest test result that showed an increase in the growth of the tumour and she became emotional. I reminded her about what she had said before and asked about any other source of support. She now mentioned her partner, the father of the child, whom she felt at her side and again she discharged. Now her right arm and leg, which were a bit dissociated initially, came to life and in the continuation of the session we explored what it was that she had held back in those parts of her body.

This simple example shows how resourcing, rather than entering an issue immediately, is an effective strategy to prevent a person from moving further into dysregulation and slowly developing the capacity to deal with a challenging or painful life situation.

Dealing with traumatic activation

After having a sense of safety and feeling resourced enough, one is now ready to deal with the traumatic event or the activation that remained unprocessed in the body. In order to do so, we should also develop our ability to track bodily sensations that tell us if we are in a state of activation, charge, discharge or relaxation. I have mentioned the physiological changes that happen during sympathetic and parasympathetic activation in the first chapter and one can learn to become sensitive to observing such changes in oneself or in another person. One can become more aware of heartbeat, breathing, hot flushes or coldness, trembling, constriction or flaccidity, muscle tension and other bodily reactions. One can teach someone to be more observant of these changes in himself. Just learning this or teaching this to a client can be helpful in moving towards a better physiological self-regulation.

For a trauma therapist, it is essential to notice any physiological changes in his client and therefore to know if the client is becoming more activated or if he is discharging. Also, emotional expressions can either be activating or relaxing, and understanding such differences can be crucial for knowing how to continue a session.

Often, we do not pay enough attention to our body while certain thoughts or inner pictures arise. In the above example, remembering her son's illness created a physical reaction in her body, an increase in her heart rate or tension in her muscles. This physiological stress response may lead to feelings of fear and anxiety, which in turn convinces the mind about the imminent danger, which leads to a further increase in heart rate or muscle constriction, as the body prepares to deal with the situation. This can start a vicious circle, where thoughts, feelings and physical reactions mutually reinforce each other, while in reality it all started with a simple thought about what *could* happen. Learning to catch a thought as a thought and watching the physical reactions as something separate from it can be a great practice in order to avoid becoming dysregulated.

Meditation

Sit with closed eyes and observe what is going on in your body. Feel your body; do not think about it or analyse what you notice, simply observe it.

Now feel your thoughts, the continuous stream of thoughts, layer upon layer of thoughts like an endless river. Some thoughts are accompanied by pleasant sensations, others by unpleasant sensations. As your thoughts change, so your sensations change. Observe this for a while, allowing your attention to shift between thoughts and physical sensations.

Now become aware that none of these thoughts are really 'yours'. They are just like clouds in the sky without any roots; they come and go and they go on changing. When you were young, there were different thoughts and now other clouds have come. You cannot really say 'my' thought.

Continue to look in and observe what happens to the feeling of 'I'.

Pendulation

When we remember a painful or frightening experience, we will often notice how our body becomes activated or a bit tense, at least if we are not completely dissociated. If we can stay with this sensation for a while, there will come a moment when this sensation begins to change as all sensations do. It may get worse or better, but it will not stay the same. There is a rhythm of expansion and contraction.

Also, awareness naturally shifts between different sensations; it moves from the pleasant to the unpleasant and back. Peter Levine has coined the term 'pendulation' to describe this natural flow that corresponds to the fact that life is always changing and moving between the pleasant and unpleasant. Pain is followed by joy and vice versa; nothing ever stays the same. In trauma, this natural flow is interrupted and a traumatised person tends to get frozen or stuck with what is unpleasant. Alternatively, in reaction, he tries to avoid it and attempts to stay only on the side of feeling good.

The intention in trauma therapy is to help a client come back from a frozen state, or from being stuck with an unpleasant sensation or feeling, to enable him to experience that change is possible and that a seemingly infinite pain can begin to be manageable and finite. The technique is to only get in touch with a small amount of activation, not get lost in it and to quickly swing back to a more pleasant experience. This back and forth movement between the traumatic memory or experience and a resource is called pendulation.

One can even view this as a general therapeutic principle: Moving between supporting or resourcing a client and challenging him, sometimes focusing on what is already going well in his life and at other times reminding him about unresolved issues. In this way he neither gets too depressed nor too ecstatic and stays grounded in reality. (I have described this in more detail in my book *The Zen Way of Counseling: A meditative approach to working with people*).

Getting in touch with a resource usually leads to a discharge and towards relaxation, while facing an unresolved conflict or trauma leads to activation. By only facing a small aspect of a traumatic experience and therefore not allowing the activation to become overwhelming, but instead by quickly moving back to the remembrance of a resource, over activation, freezing and retraumatisation are avoided and a discharge is enabled. In this way, by pendulation and continuously moving back and forth, step by step, the high charge is lowered and eventually an experience becomes digested and integrated. Slowly, the organism can move back towards self-regulation.

Titration

This process of slowly entering into trauma material and keeping the activation to a minimum is also called 'titration', which is a technical term borrowed from chemistry. There it describes the process of slowly and gradually mixing an alkaline with an acid liquid. By mixing them drop-by-drop they neutralise each other without an explosion, which would occur if they were mixed all at once. Similarly, in trauma, we are dealing with a highly explosive energy that can easily get out of control and can turn into an emotional catharsis. This often does not lead to healing and integration, but in the best case the traumatic state continues and in the worst case it can aggravate the situation and lead to symptoms of post-traumatic stress. It can be compared to the opening of a champagne bottle, which keeps the wine under pressure – when opened fast, it 'explodes' and much of the contents spill out. When, however, opened slowly and in a controlled way, the air and pressure inside can be released without creating any explosive reaction.

Similarly, in trauma therapy it is more healing to expose a client only gradually to painful and disturbing feelings and sensations. When a traumatic experience is broken down into manageable pieces, the client and his physiology have enough time to integrate and digest the experience and process the activation.

Discharge

To understand discharge, it can be helpful to observe how animals in the wild release their trapped survival energy, for example, after a fierce struggle or after returning from a play-dead reflex. Animals in the wild do not usually become traumatised even though they face threats to their lives almost daily. After coming back from a state of tonic immobility, which they entered when flight or fight were impossible, they discharge their high activation without retaining it inside their physiology. When a threat is over and the animal returns from the freeze state, it usually takes a deep breath followed by a strong shaking and trembling of the body, and the extremities move in a way that allows the unused physical energy to be released. In this way, an animal completes the original fight or flight response that was initiated and interrupted by the shock-induced paralysis.

It seems that cortical structures in human beings interfere with this reflex-like, autonomously regulated discharge. In other words, our mind overrides the spontaneous movements that are initiated from lower brain centers and stops them from being carried out. Social conditioning about what is acceptable or not sometimes interferes even more, stops us from allowing spontaneous movements of our physiology and the energy does not get released. We may all have had experiences when our body wanted to shake, maybe in fear or excitement, but when we felt that other people were watching we prevented it.

In trauma therapy, we want to give the body the opportunity to release this charge, but as the trauma response is controlled by the autonomous nervous system, only an involuntary discharge can really release the held energy. In other words, an effective discharge cannot be forced, but needs to be a spontaneous happening.

What may have helped me not to develop long lasting symptoms of post-traumatic stress was that I could allow enough emotional discharge. When driving behind the hearse, I was shouting and screaming out loud while driving my car. In another moment after the investigator had told me about the probable cause of the accident, I had gone to my hotel room and had a big catharsis, shouting and beating pillows. Constantly, for the following weeks or months, there were waves of sudden tears rolling up in me and I did not care where I was or who was around; I just allowed myself to cry or sob without being concerned about anybody. It sometimes lasted for several minutes or more until the wave of tears and crying subsided, and I always felt more peaceful afterwards.

A cathartic expression can be helpful at times if it is a spontaneous outburst rather than a voluntary effort or desire. What is often more effective is to allow a gentle discharge, because if a discharge is too intense and fierce and creates fear and overwhelm in a person, he may re-enter the state of freeze. The body may become more stressed and activated rather than discharged. Sometimes an emotional expression can feel like a relief in the beginning, but can later turn into an activation. Clients, as well as therapists, have to observe this carefully. Usually, a spontaneous discharge lasts briefly and then stops, while expressions arising from habit can last a long time and drain our energy.

Only when the discharge involves the brainstem and is involuntary can it complete the incomplete responses of fight and flight. Once we are able to allow our body to do this, we emerge from a state of collapse towards a state of empowerment; we become energised and can move out of the survival mode in which we were stuck. Now other brain structures like the limbic system come online, and social engagement and contact with others becomes possible again.

Anger and fear are related to fight and flight responses and are part of nature's way of helping us survive. People who are traumatised are often unable to contact their healthy aggression; they either cannot access anger or have sudden explosive outbursts that they cannot control. On the other hand, they are sometimes unable to feel when they are putting themselves in danger; they remain frozen and paralysed when attacked or criticised, unable to defend themselves or remove themselves from a dangerous and unhealthy situation.

There are various anger exercises that one can practice that are helpful in discovering healthy aggression and becoming comfortable with feeling anger. Anger can energise our body, mobilise our energy for action and give us strength and vitality to pursue our life purpose. But it is also helpful to learn to respect fear as part of our biological intelligence, as this is the way our body wants to show us that it would be better to leave a situation and find a safer place.

Feelings of anger or fear usually increase when we perceive that we cannot defend ourselves or cannot escape. It is the way our body tries to move us into action. Once we start to defend ourselves or escape, the emotion is usually reduced. That is the reason why in a traumatic situation, where neither fight or escape are possible and these impulses remain frozen and incomplete inside our body, people often feel overwhelmed with anger and rage or fear and panic. This frozenness can only dissolve when we begin to learn and feel confident that we can defend ourselves or leave a situation when necessary. That is the reason why it is so important to learn how to feel safe, but also to be in contact with one's strength and ability to fight.

Healthy aggression exercise

With a partner: *Stand opposite each other and put one or both hands against your partner's hand. One partner starts to push while the other resists. Take it easy, not too intense and take a break whenever you have had enough. Take turns with who is pushing and who is resisting.*

Experiment with making eye contact.

You can also experiment with making angry faces at each other, but remember not to get serious. Make sure you do not collapse or overdo. Try to discover when you feel a strengthening in your body. It is not about going into emotional catharsis or a competition about who is stronger.

You can do the same exercise while pushing against your partner's back. Again, take turns with who is pushing and who is resisting.

Without a partner: *If you do not have someone to do this exercise with, you can try to practice pushing with your hands or back against a wall.*

Integration

In dealing with traumatic experiences, it is especially important to allow enough integration time, so the body and mind can process and reorganise themselves before dealing with new material. Slowing things down and waiting until an experience is absorbed prevents overstimulation.

Frequently, clients want to heal fast and overcome a state of fear quickly, or they can have a tendency to overestimate their own capacity about what they can handle and as a consequence put too much pressure on themselves. This can further increase the activation of their already overcharged state and fail to allow their system to calm down. When we learn to truly love ourselves, we will not do anything that is too much or too fast for our body.

Education

Clients often do not realise how much pressure they put on themselves and frequently are not in touch with the needs of their own body. Educating them about how the body functions, what happens in trauma and how to support the body in dealing with symptoms, is an essential element in preparing someone to take better care of himself and perceive the body as a friend. If we understand what our body is trying to do for us, even when a symptom is disturbing, we can begin to support our body rather than fighting with it. For example, learning something about what a panic attack is, what leads to it and what is helpful in dealing with it, can help a person to pay more attention to early signals and this can become a first step in rediscovering lost control. It can also be a relief from the shame of not being able to control certain symptoms.

Generally, a therapist's attitude should be to give support to the body rather than to the mind. Our mind is often in a hurry to reach somewhere, while our body needs time. Educating our mind about the ways of the body can create an understanding and support for what our body needs from us in order to heal.

Apart from Family Constellation, where there is nothing particular to do for a client after a session and we only give one session, working with the body sometimes needs a series of sessions. It can also be useful to give some practical homework to a client in between sessions, so a new skill or understanding can be practiced.

Meditation

Sit or stand comfortably and close your eyes. Watch the rise and fall of your breath and imagine it as a pendulum moving from left to right and right to left.

Now observe your thoughts and feelings as if they too are a pendulum moving from pleasure to pain, from happiness to unhappiness, back and forth, on and on. Sometimes this movement is slow and sometimes faster, but everything changes to its opposite.

Now put your attention neither on pleasure nor on pain, but between these.

Usually our mind clings to a happy moment and wants to escape from an unhappy moment. Now don't cling to happiness and do not try to get rid of unhappiness, just be the witness of both. Remember, if pain is there, sooner or later it is going to go and when happiness has come it will also not stay.

Remain a witness to both and be in the middle.

(Meditation taken from Vigyan Bhairav Tantra Vol I, A new commentary by Osho, #59)

Example from a session

A female client comes with the issue of insomnia. She also reports that she struggles with a recurring feeling of shame. Initially, it shows that she is dissociated from some parts of her body and she mentions that her muscles feel flaccid. Her physical energy is rather collapsed, so we deal with a collapsed type of shame.

Rather than immediately resourcing her, I ask her to observe her body sensations and any feelings that arise as we explore the body. She now also mentions that she had dyslexia as a child. Remembering this creates some activation in her and as we explore this, she connects with an impulse of wanting to push with her arms, which I invite her to follow.

In the first part of this session, we mainly work with her body and follow how it goes in and out of a state of collapse. When she moves into collapse, she also notices feelings of wanting to cry and when she connects with the impulse to push and move her arms, she becomes aware of anger. Gradually, she starts to enjoy her defensive fight response that brings her out of shame. In this way, she learns that feeling shame and collapsed is time limited; it comes and goes and can change. We practice following and enjoying the impulse to push and being aware whenever she needs to rest and relax her efforts.

In the next part of the session, we work more directly with her anger towards her teacher, who was strict and not supportive when she was dyslexic, but rather pressured her and enhanced her feeling that something was wrong with her. Now we pendulate between the anger towards her teacher and the fear of her. We look for a resource and examine the relationship to her parents, who were working a lot and not very available for support. This missing resource made it difficult for her to deal with her teacher. Moreover, her symptom was also an unconscious cry for more attention that did not succeed. I ask her what she would have needed from her mother and after she mentions that she wanted her mother to hold her, I ask her to imagine her mother standing close to her as a support (fantasy resource). As she softens and allows some tears, she now connects with her own sensitivity that she was not in touch with as she was under so much pressure and effort to be 'good', which obviously being dyslexic she failed to fulfil.

Now she feels more empowered, more able to face her teacher and also capable of enjoying her anger without so quickly going into collapse. Gradually, the vitality also spreads to her legs and as she moves both arms and legs, she feels more energised. Also, her voice has more energy now. We not only focus on expression, but also on observing how the feeling of having inner space grows. Slowly she learns to face her teacher with calmness, telling her how she felt not treated well.

Eventually she can acknowledge what she missed as a child from both her teacher and her parents and after completing her unexpressed feelings towards them, especially her anger and disappointment, she feels empowered and calmer. The attitude of holding her energy back had contributed to her childhood dyslexia and also to her prolonged symptom of sleeplessness. Both symptoms relate to a held back charge.

This session was followed by a Family Constellation session where we explored why her parents could not support her more and in what way her anger was not only personal, but also systemic and taken over for her father, which gave a deeper insight into the symptom of insomnia.

Chapter Seven

The Systemic Approach to Healing Trauma

While working with systemic and trans-generational trauma, Family Constellation offers no guidelines on how a traumatised client should be treated differently from other clients. This can possibly lead to a kind of neglect of the fact that traumatised clients do sometimes need to be treated in ways that differ from other clients. As explained in the previous chapters, clients who suffer from trauma need to be exposed to the memory of a traumatic event and the unprocessed energy it generated more slowly; they need to feel especially safe and resourced and generally need to be given more time for integration.

Even if all the systemic entanglements that led to a traumatic event and the roots in the family system are understood, this still may not lead to relief of the related symptoms. We have described how the physiological mechanism that is responsible for trauma symptoms is governed by a part of the brain that has not yet realised that the threat is over, and this means that intellectual knowledge alone will have no or almost no transforming effect.

In order for any trauma therapy to be effective, it needs to address and influence those primitive brain structures that keep a person fixated in the past. A completion needs to happen in our physiology. And this will also influence our feelings, beliefs and way of thinking. If a constellation is to be effective, it needs to reach those parts of our mind and brain; even reaching to the emotional level may not be sufficient.

This is the main reason why I consider the new approach of constellation work, where representatives are not asked to speak or share what they experience, to have a much deeper effect when dealing with trauma. Too much talking and analysing in a session engages our intellect, but leaves deeper layers of our psyche untouched. To only know something intellectually about a subject is not an insight and has no transformative effect. Insight is sudden and comes as a surprise, as if a light has been switched on and suddenly all is clear. Intellectual knowledge is the result of exploring and studying a subject; it often involves effort and takes time. Knowledge is sometimes meaningful as it opens our mind to a subject and prepares us to enter a process or experience, but it is only the experience itself that really matters and leads to transformation. If the experience is missing, all knowledge is futile. This means that a session needs to give a client a new experience and not only new information.

Completing the past needs to happen for body, heart and mind simultaneously. In a constellation, we need to sense on a physical level what is going on in our body and how the body wants to move. We consciously need to come into touch with the hidden love and sometimes this also involves understanding with whom from our family system we are identified. But even if this understanding is missing and we only follow how the energy field moves us, it is often enough for healing.

For example, when a mother who has lost her child looks at the dead body, no words need to be uttered and no explanation given, during or after the constellation. To just give space for whatever wants to happen in the moment is probably the most appropriate. The mother may want to lie down next to her child, or hold her child, or cry or become angry. There are many possible ways in which an individual might deal with such a traumatic event and they are all meaningful. When someone is able to fully allow whatever arises from inside, this will eventually lead a person to where life wants to take them.

The new approach to Family Constellation

While originally in a Family Constellation session, representatives were positioned by the client, then asked about their feelings in their position and eventually moved to another, more 'rightful' place within the system by the therapist; the later approach to Family Constellation works more with spontaneous movements of the representatives. They are randomly chosen from a group, sometimes not even told whom they represent, and often placed anywhere in an open space and then asked to follow their inner impulses. In this way, some hidden relationship dynamics between the members of the systemic field are brought to light, including what moves inside a person's personal and collective unconscious mind. Allowing a constellation to be guided only by the impulses of the representatives comes very close to body-oriented trauma therapy, where we work with the felt sense and try to follow and respect bodily signals.

Example from a session

A man lost his brother in a sudden car accident in childhood and is still very affected by this traumatic experience. When facing his brother in a constellation, he moves through many physical and emotional responses that are still incomplete and unexpressed inside of him. He is given time to process his feelings of anger, pain and despair. Nothing is said, only another representative for the bus that killed his brother, is added to the constellation. He watches as his brother is being hugged by that representative, eventually lying down and resting in that representative's lap. Slowly, he also hugs his brother and then finally gets up and stands alone and by himself, realising his own life path and new direction.

Without any spoken words, the client in this constellation went through similar physiological and emotional movements that one would expect to see in a somatic trauma session, while at the same time, through a lived experience, he learns to move forward and learns about conscious love that takes one beyond bonding.

If an intellectual explanation of what happened is sometimes given at the end of such a session, the purpose is only to appease the mind, because the real healing happens through witnessing the movements themselves. There is an intrinsic movement within all systems towards healing and moving out of the frozen state of trauma.

How trauma shows in a constellation

As we discussed, one-way trauma shows in the body is through frozenness, dissociation and being unable to socially engage. In a similar way, we see frozenness in constellations when representatives are unable to move or to look at one another, or they are unable to relate and see someone for who they really are.

There are no definite criteria for calling such a situation traumatic rather than just painful. It is generally difficult to clearly distinguish between the two, but there are life events that tend to be traumatic and overwhelming for everyone. Ultimately, only a person's individual reaction to an event and whether his body is able to regulate the activation can decide whether it can be called traumatic. Trauma is really related to the inner experience of an event, not to the event itself. This can make it more challenging to bring back flow and aliveness into a person's life and repair his ability to relate with others. It is then often not enough to only do a constellation, but some work with the physiology needs to be included.

There are various ways to create movement in a constellation. First, we try to bring some missing people into the systemic field – someone who was forgotten, rejected, left out, ignored or judged. When the right person is found and added to the field, others will begin to move or get in touch with an emotion. Secondly, we help a person to establish his own boundaries and step out of someone else's energy field. For example, if a child is too close to his parents and tries to help them, he is not able to live his own life and will tend to be overwhelmed by what he is trying to do and by the emotions and the trauma he is carrying for his parents. Everyone in a family has his 'rightful' place that belongs to him alone. Unresolved trauma leads to entanglements, where a person tries to involve himself in the life of someone else. It creates confusion, disorder and boundary violation.

Let's imagine a situation where a client lost his mother early in life and during childhood was unable to process the emotions related to that loss and never fully recovered from the shock. Instead, he remained in the defence strategy of forgetting what happened and therefore not remembering his mother. Unconsciously, however, the longing for the mother remains unfulfilled and as a consequence he keeps looking for a mother in other people, maybe in his partner or child.

If he has children himself, one of them may have the tendency to carry the pain of this parent in an effort to relieve him of it. In a constellation, this may be visible by the representative for the client either turning away from his present family, looking for someone else, or he may look at his partner or child, but is unable to see them for who they really are. So, two things happen: there is a missing person, the mother who died early, and there is disorder or confusion of boundaries.

When we place a representative for the real mother into the constellation in front of the representative for the client, he will most likely feel drawn to her or come in contact with the undigested pain of losing her. By experiencing these feelings now, they are processed and the energy that kept them locked in the unconscious is freed up. Then his own child is freed of the need to do anything for his parent. Also he becomes able to see his own child or partner clearly for the first time. Now the capacity to relate to his family in a healthier way is re-established and there is movement and flow in the relationships, where coming closer or moving apart become possible.

In systemic work, we do not allow a client to regress into the state of *being* a child, but while feeling his childhood pain we also ask him to remember his present state and not get lost in the old wound. In this way, a psychological completion of an unfinished event from the past can be achieved. This also affects the body, which then can move out of a frozen or dissociated state, and tears are one of the main ways to process and heal old wounds and losses.

This example is very simple, but it illustrates that healing requires us to face a traumatic event from the past, feel its impact on our life and acknowledge the love we have or had for a certain person. Through systemic work, we can see that this relates not only to our personal experiences, but also to those of other family members. To uncover that hidden love is not always easy and we sometimes have to pass through anger, frustration, panic or pain, and accept the need to find support.

Honouring parents and ancestors

In trauma, our ability to defend ourselves is overwhelmed and as a consequence we often remain stuck in a defensive response, which shows up in an automatic tendency to say 'no' to someone or something. A person who feels capable of saying 'no' is not defensive, because he is unafraid. If a traumatic experience is related to our parents, we might become stuck in an attitude of rejection or complaint against them. To teach such a client that he needs to honour his parents may be useless, possibly even harmful, because he first needs to find a way to complete his defence response, including allowing feelings of anger or fear. The impulse in children to defend themselves is often in conflict with the impulse to bond, which is the reason why children can easily become frozen, unable to come closer to their parents or move away from them. Before they can find genuine respect and love, both these natural impulses need to be acknowledged and completed. To impose an idea of respect from the very beginning may not be helpful, but could instead become a new conditioning.

So, a facilitator of Family Constellation needs to remember that love and respect should arise from a client's growing awareness and cannot be enforced from outside. Authentic respect can only come when one also feels the inner freedom and capacity to say 'no' when necessary. A true 'yes' is not a collapse or a giving up. A traumatic event by definition means that our energy collapsed or shut down, and by connecting to our fight or flight responses we become capable of moving out of this collapsed or frozen state. Only after completing this reconnection are we able to feel love towards our parents or others family members and truly honour them.

In English, the word 'respect' literally means 'looking again' – 're-spect'. It means to look at the other with awareness and see him or her as he or she is. When we are burdened with emotional wounds from the past, we cannot see the reality of the other. We are still too involved in our own dreams and projections that originated from an undigested past. After facing these wounds and passing through any unpleasant feelings that may arise, some inner clarity emerges and then we become able to experience authentic respect and love.

In a constellation, the reality of a parent or any other family member becomes clear, and it is possible to see and understand why they could not fulfil our childhood expectations. Children usually either idealise or demonise their parents and we often continue this tendency into adulthood, not only towards our parents, but towards many of the people with whom we relate. This shows that a trauma from the past has not been processed and we have not become able to look at each other realistically.

At some point, all children are disappointed with their parents and as they grow up, they have to learn to tolerate frustration. But whether they can learn this easily or not depends on whether they were disappointed too frequently or too early during their upbringing. Again, this depends on whether their parents managed to handle and overcome their own disappointments and traumas.

Learning to let go of unrealistic ideas and expectations about one's parents and not get stuck in the unconscious hope that one day they will be fulfilled is not an easy task and the more trauma there is in a system, the more challenging it will be. Parents are in reality ordinary people, as everyone is, neither terrible nor great, and have many unresolved traumas of their own.

The approach of Family Constellation is very down to earth and tries to move us out of our dreams, so we can look at life as it is, accepting our parents and all other family members as they are. When we achieve this, we are connected to an authentic strength, inner clarity and love all at the same time.

When we bow to a parent or to someone else in a constellation, this is not a movement of submission, but a symbolic gesture of love and respect. This only has meaning and significance when it comes from the awareness of what the other has done for us and what they have gone through in their life. Only then does this gesture have a special beauty and grace; it cannot be done out of will, but comes as our consciousness reaches a certain point.

Parents are a child's greatest resource and at the same time can cause many traumas. Remembering what our parents have done for us in this life, that they gave birth to us and took care of us for many years, will create a sense of gratitude towards them. Remembering what we didn't get from them and how they were not there when we needed them or even hurt us, will cause different feelings. To be realistic, we need to acknowledge both and make space for all our feelings. Then we eventually come to understand the existential fact that life is dual – it sometimes supports us and sometimes challenges us. We are helpless and on the receiving end and nothing is ever in our hands. Unknowingly, the painful can also support our journey to higher consciousness.

Visualisation

Sit comfortably with closed eyes. Imagine that you are looking at one of your parents, or anyone from your life with whom you feel you have some unfinished business. Hold the image of this person in front of your inner eye.

Allow yourself to feel whatever comes up within you, include any memories and experiences you had with this person.

After a while, imagine letting yourself see what is behind the other person, imagine that you are looking through them, as if they are transparent. You might see different people, or events that have happened. Continue looking until you see a bright light or a big energy behind everything and everyone; you do not exactly know what it is.

Notice any changes within you.

In a session, I sometimes ask a client to stand in front of a parent for a long time and wait until an inner movement starts to happen. In the beginning, he may only be aware of complaints and rejections, remembering all the wounds and the things he didn't receive, but after a while, other feelings start to appear and he may connect with a layer of love underneath. This love is never really absent, only covered by layers of dust, of unfulfilled desires. In reality, we have no choice; we all love our parents and family members and we are programmed by nature to bond.

One intention of a constellation is to connect us again with this bonding love. Once we are in contact with it, the further learning will be to rise above it and find a more conscious love. These are the two learning steps of every constellation: To admit to the bonding love and then to learn to move beyond it.

As we all have the tendency to be too focused on the negative, on what is missing and what we did not receive, it can be meaningful to consciously ask ourselves what it was that we *did* receive. This step is difficult to do when one is in the trauma state, but it can help us to connect with a sense of gratitude and then processing old wounds is much easier and less overwhelming.

Exercise

Make a list of what you did receive from your mother and father or from anyone in your life against whom you still hold a grudge.

When we see the history of our family and the previous lives of parents, grandparents and other ancestors in a constellation, we realise that we come into this life as part of a great chain, that nobody really did anything on his own, but life happened to everyone in a certain way that did not allow him much choice. Understanding this can make us humbler and help us to give up the self-importance that in some ways we still carry within us since childhood. We learn to be less demanding and more accepting of our life destiny, and to enjoy the small things during our short life span.

Learning to loosen the bonding ties with our family and to take life into our own hands means giving up the idea that anybody owes us anything. This is one of the main objectives of a Family Constellation session. Freedom always comes with self-responsibility.

Parents are not only here for their children; they also have their own lives and when children become adults, they need to learn to leave their parents. The idea of 'my' parent or 'my' child or 'my' partner is an illusion that we need to let go of. We can learn this through meditation and Family Constellation, conducted in this way, prepares us for such an understanding.

Trauma and Narcissism

As a toddler, everybody goes through a developmental stage called the 'narcissistic stage', during which he sees himself as the center of the universe, and others are only there to fulfil his needs. If during that stage he suffers either neglect or indulgence, he is not able to complete that stage successfully and leave it behind, so he fails to learn about his own and other people's boundaries. This can happen if parents excessively praise their child as being special, but without any warmth, or alternatively if they neglect him. This leads to the development of the so-called narcissistic personality, very different from the healthy self-esteem that develops when a child has received love and warmth and is confirmed and mirrored as being good and beautiful.

When, for example, a mother has to raise her children during wartime or in other traumatic circumstances, she may not be able to respond appropriately to these fundamental needs of her child. Then the child, who does not feel loved and cared for, or is not shown where his own limits are, may either develop a sense that something is basically wrong with him, or he may develop a narcissistic personality, or he may become a 'hero', sacrificing himself for his mother and others.

Children naturally trust their parents and cannot imagine that anything is wrong with them. Nor are they capable of understanding their parents' complex and sometimes traumatic life situations. When they are not receiving the right kind of care and mirroring, they tend to think they are wrong or unworthy. When later in life such a child has children of his own, he will pass onto them whatever he did or did not receive. He may even want from his children the love and appreciation he had missed from his parents. In this way, traumas are passed on from one generation to the next. There is really no point at which it all started. Everyone has to process not only his own traumas, but also those of his parents and former family members. Our life is built on the lives of all those who came before us from former generations.

When in a constellation we see and understand the complex and traumatic life situation our mother was in, then our feelings towards her might change as we start to realise that she actually did all she could to support us. Then we no longer feel as if we missed anything, but suddenly come into contact with the love that we longed for. In reality, love does not come from outside, but wells up from within. The same life situation starts to appear different and, rather than looking like a deficiency, can become a resource. That is the magic that can happen in a constellation session. And it is possible to experience this in relation to all the members of our extended family.

When our judgements drop and, in their place, love arises in our hearts, we will feel enriched and strengthened. But this has to be a real insight, not just intellectual knowledge.

It can be a delicate matter to take a client out of a childhood dream or to challenge a narcissistic personality. When a person feels overly disturbed, he could become shocked again and an old tendency could be strengthened rather than healed. Healing happens not just by reliving a past event, but by receiving the right support in order to successfully pass through old disappointments and frustrations. The somatic trauma approach offers insights and tools for helping clients to digest unresolved childhood traumas without becoming retraumatised, overwhelmed or dissociated. As Family Constellation does not really distinguish trauma from other painful events, facilitators may ignore the importance of treating traumatised clients in a specific way.

For this reason, I find it necessary to add a somatic understanding to the work of Family Constellation. I will suggest here how some of the principles of a somatic approach that we discussed in the previous chapter could be applied to a systemic constellation:

Resourcing

A traumatised client is often not fully able to realise that he also received love. Helping him to see that is a way of resourcing him during a constellation. Rather than facing a traumatic event directly, it is often better to focus first on the support that was available, however small it may have been. Sometimes it is only afterwards that one can come out of a frozen state and allow one's feelings.

In the case of an early death, the missing person in the constellation is often not only the one who died, but often those who stayed alive and, for example, supported the child and took care of him. It is important that they are acknowledged and not forgotten too.

Example from a session

A male client lost his father early in life when he was only five. In the constellation his representative looked at the floor, but was unable to move or feel anything when the dead father was placed on the floor. When his mother was brought in, initially he did not look at her. After she processed her own tears and shock about losing her husband, she then turned to her son. When the son then also looked at her, he could go to his mother and she hugged him. Only now could he also cry while looking at his father again and begin to process his loss.

A child who loses a parent early usually needs the resource of the living parent in order to process and digest his loss. Without feeling the love and support of the caretaker, who stayed with the child and continued to bring him up, the early loss of a parent cannot be digested. Sometimes, when the living parent is unable to recover from the loss of his or her partner, it is then almost as if the child lost both his parents at the same time and it becomes difficult to overcome the trauma.

Sometimes, there is more trauma in one branch of the family system than in the other. Then the therapist has to choose which part of the system to work with. Usually one would focus where the biggest entanglement is, but in the case of severe trauma it is often better to first work with the part of the system from where more support and love can flow towards the client. In other words, the therapist first needs to help the client to come into touch with being loved before he can face how the trauma on the other side of his family has affected him.

There are situations where both father and mother carry so much trauma that their child feels that he wants to die. Then, sometimes only by connecting to other siblings (if there are any), or by placing a representative for life, can he feel a sense of wanting to stay alive or find any joy. Finding resources for a client who is dealing with severe trauma is also an important principle in systemic work. Guiding questions can be: Who was able to support, love and take care of the client during childhood or when facing a traumatic situation? What did the client actually receive that was supportive? What other aspects of a situation or what personal abilities helped a client to pass through a trauma or difficult life period?

Titration

This principle can be applied to any kind of therapeutic session when dealing with traumatic content, to avoid overstimulation. A client can be asked to talk slowly, allowing gaps between sentences and taking deep breaths, or he can be asked to talk about one event at a time rather than mentioning a whole series of painful events all at the same time. It is important to break the tendency in traumatised clients to constantly overstimulate themselves. Bert Hellinger, the founder of Family Constellation, sometimes allowed a client to utter only one sentence, which could also be viewed as a way to help him to focus and contain his energy.

A constellation can even be conducted with no initial talk. But I like to give traumatised clients the feeling that they have some control over what is happening in their session and also respect their need to express themselves. By explaining to a client why he is asked to talk about only one event at a time and not rush into 'telling the whole story', he also learns to understand and assess his own process.

In a system with multiple traumas, it is often good to choose only one event to deal with in a session and leave other issues for another moment. It may even be good for traumatised clients not to look at the most challenging event, but rather to deal with something less frightening, even if this is not the main cause of the problem. It is like any form of training – better to go slowly, to tackle something minor at first before approaching a more challenging issue. This is contrary to the usual idea that one should always go immediately to the root of a problem.

Pendulation

Pendulation describes the natural movement between contraction and expansion. When facing a trauma we contract, when feeling loved we expand. Staying in contraction and being unable to come out of it and expand again is a symptom of trauma – just as at the other extreme one clings onto the feeling of expansion and tries to avoid the contraction. When we remember what our parents did for us, we expand, but when we remember what they could not, we contract. Both are reality. The work of a session is to re-establish a person's ability to move between the two; in other words, to be able to flow with the ups and downs of life.

In our example from above, the client was focusing on his dead father and could not see his mother – he became stuck and frozen. In other situations, a person may only see his mother and may want to replace the father, therefore avoiding him. In either situation, we want to create an oscillating movement between feeling the support of one parent while at some point facing the absence of the other. If a client becomes frozen or goes into shock, we look for support and when he feels too elated, we remind him about the pain he also needs to deal with. Pain can be a very grounding and humbling experience and when a person becomes able to see both parents together, he becomes balanced.

In a session, a therapist may ask a client to look back and forth between the two parents, seeing both alternately without choosing one over the other. The problem for children always arises when parents ask them to choose one over the other and children often solve this conflict by following one of them outwardly, but inwardly following the other. If a mother does not want her son to become like his father, he will outwardly agree with his mother and reject his father, but in life he will start behaving like his father.

Life is always the totality of two alternatives and the moment we choose only one, we create a dichotomy inside. In an angry person, fear is hidden and in a fearful person anger is hidden. In order to become whole, we need to bring the hidden side out into the open. This is one of the objectives of therapy.

Discharge

Discharge simply means releasing an energy that we were holding back. This is part of almost any form of therapy, yet the way this is done varies. It can be subtle or cathartic, emotional or just physical. While discharging, a client may give a deep out breath, laugh, smile, start crying or shaking, get angry or be moved in other ways. Typically, the discharge in a constellation shows when a representative starts to cry or express other emotions that he has been holding back. After allowing it, he usually feels relief and again becomes able to move, either closer or further away from someone. When we move out of being identified with someone, we start seeing the other as if for the first time. Then a real and conscious connection is established rather than only an unconscious bond.

It is important to distinguish between different emotional expressions. One we call **primary emotion**, which takes us into new territory and we feel something we have not felt before. The other is called **secondary emotion**. This is a more familiar emotional expression that hides another emotion underneath. We may cry when we are really angry, or laugh when we feel embarrassed, or get angry when we really feel hurt. Secondary emotions are like a default response, something we do automatically when anything is touched in us. In therapy, we want to support primary emotions and discourage secondary emotions. Secondary emotions are frequent after trauma and they often lead to a state of collapse – they really weaken a person. Afterwards, we feel exhausted, while after a primary emotion we usually feel strengthened and more alive.

We often discover in a constellation that the client's pain is actually not his own, but the pain of someone else from the family that he took over. For example, someone might cry for his mother while the mother herself does not feel anything. In a session, he may be asked to leave this pain to his mother and if he can do that his tears immediately stop or become less. Then the mother will feel the pain and his learning will be to leave it to his mother and tolerate seeing her in pain. He may cry a little bit with her, because we are all bonded and we love our mother and her sadness also makes us a little bit sad. But it is not like trying to save her from it. There is a great difference between crying *for* one's mother or *with* one's mother. Moreover, this kind of sadness does not have an overwhelming quality; it is appropriate and comes with our life and with the fact that we are part of a particular family. When a representative has a dramatic emotional expression, it is usually a sign that he is not expressing his own feelings, but the feelings of someone else. Such dramatic outbursts are often related to unhealed traumas – often it is not a personal trauma, but the trauma of another family member. For traumatised clients, it is helpful to minimise a discharge and emotional expression, so it does not lead to a state of overwhelm. A relieving emotional expression can very quickly become activating and move out of control.

Integration

After a constellation, it is helpful to give enough time for integration, to allow space to feel what happened in the constellation rather than trying to process more or explore further. The mind is usually greedy in the sense that it wants to achieve more; it has a goal that it wants to reach. Growth, however, is a slow process that needs patience and time. Just because we want to solve a problem, it does not mean that we can solve it. Traumatised clients are often not in touch with their own limits and compensate for their feeling of having lost control by overestimating their capacity to process more.

Life is a subtle balance, where 'bigger' events are always beyond our ability to control them, unlike 'smaller' events. When we adopt a humble attitude towards life and accept helplessness as a basic human condition, we also expand the ability to allow discomfort and conflict in our life without an attitude of having to 'fix' it. Then we can also give more space and time for integration in our lives.

It is often better to look at only one entanglement at a time, to stay connected to a certain insight for a while and to avoid a long talk or analysis after a constellation has ended. Silent intervals with no talking are a main ingredient of any session that has depth and a therapist needs to learn to allow and be comfortable with moments of not knowing what to do next.

After a constellation has ended and a client returns from being in the systemic field, it can be important to check if he has arrived back in the here and now, after having encountered events and memories from the past. Grounding through the body, creating eye contact and talking about the present moment life situation can support this.

In Chapter Eleven, we will also talk about creativity and orienting someone towards the future. I sometimes remind a client of a new resource he has found during the session and help him track through the body the effect this has on him right now. It is often good not to analyse the session or ask a client if he understood what happened in the constellation, as this brings a person back into the neo-cortical circuits.

Standing Meditation

While standing with closed eyes, feel what is behind your back and what has happened in your life or in the life of your family in the past. There are traumatic and also many joyful events and moments. Give yourself some time to feel this and notice in what way this still affects you right now.

After a while, notice the big space in front of you, as if you are looking towards an unknown future and all that is going to happen to you, without you being aware of what this will be and how it will unfold. Give yourself some time to notice how this makes you feel.

Now become aware of where you and your body are right now. Feel the floor beneath your feet and the subtle movement of your breath and heartbeat. Notice the tiny present moment that you have right now and that instantly becomes a past moment. It is like sand running through your fingers. You cannot hold it, only watch what is happening. Notice the witnessing consciousness that knows no past or future.

Chapter Eight

A Somatic Family Constellation Approach

In the previous chapters, I gave a summary of the somatic trauma therapy called 'Somatic Experiencing'. I have also described how one can use this understanding in a Family Constellation session in order to treat traumatised clients in a different way from other clients. Such a session remains only a constellation session, where one does not specifically work with the body and its physiological activation. In this chapter, I will suggest how a bodily and systemic approach can be used within one single session to make the session more effective and more profound for a client.

Only if one can reach all levels of being, body, mind and heart, can an unresolved trauma be brought to a completion and a person's capacity to flow with life and be in contact with himself and his social surroundings be restored. Although when working with the body it is not always necessary to know the exact details of a traumatic event, when we work systemically, we often investigate the issue or the client's family background. One could call the first way, starting with the felt sense, a 'bottom up' approach, and the second, where we change our beliefs and the way we look at events, a 'top down' approach. It is often important to combine both approaches.

Before we look at some examples of how this could be accomplished, I will discuss what could be possibly missed when only working in one direction.

What a Family Constellation can overlook

Most people have a tendency to avoid dealing with what has been painful in their past and it is this load of an incomplete past that prevents a person from living in the present. However, not all painful events are necessarily traumatic and while trauma therapy tends to treat everyone as if he has been traumatised, systemic therapy may not give enough importance to how devastating a trauma can be for our body and that this needs to be considered before beginning to do a constellation. For example, the work should be less confrontational, or a traumatic episode should not be approached too directly in order to avoid any retraumatisation. This can mean that it may not be a helpful intervention to place a perpetrator opposite his victim from the very beginning of a constellation session, as is commonly done in systemic work. The intention to initiate a healing movement between them may need a more subtle preparation in order to avoid reactivating the original freeze response.

 I have observed constellations where the client, who was watching the movements of the representatives, became increasingly dissociated and in the end, when asked by the therapist if he 'understood', he nodded his head and returned to his place in a dazed state. He may have understood something intellectually or only wanted to please the therapist, but in either case his entire body-mind was obviously not involved in what had happened during the constellation and he remained in a state of dissociation. Unless a constellation brings a client in deep contact with love, nothing of significance has happened. Authentic love touches us on various levels; it reaches the heart and also affects our body. To distinguish whether the love is real or only a belief, a facilitator needs to remain aware of his client's physical reactions while he continues to work with the representatives in a constellation.

Pacing the body is a way to be in tune with a client's process and this is sometimes missed if a systemic therapist is overly identified with systemic knowledge about how 'right' relating between family members should look. Without examining a situation and having a direct experience, all knowledge is bound to become a block, it cannot become someone's 'knowing'.

Teaching can easily turn into another conditioning about the right way of living and may even lead to more repression. For example, I would not start a session by asking a client to bow to his parents or repeat some pre-formulated healing sentences, if this is not related to a client's growing understanding about what his parents have done for him – something that is more likely to happen towards the end of a session. Love and respect cannot be imposed, but happen spontaneously when our awareness reaches a certain level. Before we can drop unrealistic expectations about our parents, we have to first pass through pain, anger and disappointment. We also need to acknowledge that it was painful when our childhood needs were not fulfilled. It is only after the defensive response of our body has been brought to a completion that true understanding and reconciliation with parents becomes possible.

I often encourage a client to stay with his anger towards a parent, if this is truer for him, rather than asking him to say 'thank you' or to bow in an inauthentic way. Remaining true to oneself and at the same time bringing awareness to a situation, will eventually lead to reconciliation. True anger is also part of love.

Example from a session

A client shares that he really loves and respects his mother. After I place a representative for him in front of a representative for his mother, his representative after a while begins to clench his fists. I give him the sentence to say to his mother: "I want to kill you". Without further comment, we end the small exploration.

What a somatic approach may overlook

In a somatic trauma work, we mainly deal with personal trauma and its effects on the physiology. In some cases, it is also important to examine in what way one has unconsciously contributed to the traumatic event, or even created it. A purely somatic approach may overlook this fact. Of course, this is not always the case, but we know from systemic work that sometimes children are identified with former family members and have a wish to die in order to save another family member. As a consequence, they unconsciously seek situations that endanger their life or well-being. Unless the unconscious bonds that are at the root of tragic events are also examined and one is not only focused on physiological healing, the danger is that similar situations will be endlessly recreated.

Daughters whose mothers were raped, may get into abusive situations in their lives repeatedly. Sons whose fathers were in the war, may want to die for them. I have explained three main systemic patterns that lead to suffering: following, taking over and atoning for guilt.

If these patterns are not brought to the light of consciousness, especially in the case of childhood traumas, then somatic healing alone may have limited effects. A holistic healing approach will deal with the personal and physiological effects of trauma and at the same time address hidden bonding issues that have deep roots in the traumas of other members of a family or social group, sometimes from former generations.

A purely somatic approach can underestimate the power of bonding. People often unconsciously choose to suffer, which we often see in constellation work. We carry the feeling of self-importance from childhood into our adult life and may either blame ourselves excessively and feel guilty for a tragic event or seek for someone else to blame, even if an event was just part of life. To live without explanation is often hard. Only consciousness and understanding of circumstances that are not part of the body can take one beyond biological survival responses and bonding needs.

We are born with the impulse to defend ourselves and to bond with others, to self-regulate and to co-regulate. In healing, we need to acknowledge and negotiate *both* these inner drives and if only one of them is satisfied, the other is bound to take revenge. If we seek to be free from our parents without feeling love for them as well, we find ourselves in a cul-de-sac, and it is the same for those who sacrifice their own lives for the sake of their parents.

Sometimes somatic trauma therapists overly resource a client without examining if this is really needed. Rather than helping a client to find his inner strength, this can weaken him, as it can lead to anxiousness and self-doubt. There are people who have done a lot of somatic trauma therapy who develop a tendency to feel overly sensitive and fearful of being overwhelmed. Discovering and being grounded in one's own resources and connected to one's own strength does not happen only by receiving support; it needs confrontation and challenge as well. Of course, this needs to be judged according to a client's inner resilience. Being overly cared for can be as harmful as being overly challenged.

The purpose of providing a sense of safety for a client is only to counteract his loss of safety when the trauma happened. So, it should only be a temporary measure that provides the possibility of digesting a difficult experience and making him more capable of handling the general insecurity of life. Our body and mind strive for safety, but existentially this cannot be fulfilled, neither physiologically nor psychologically, as body and mind are going to die and disappear eventually.

Early childhood traumas particularly cannot be healed only on a physiological level and the consciousness of the adult needs to be addressed as well. A small child whose mother died will simply experience her sudden absence and may respond with anger, feeling as if the mother showed that she did not love her child by abandoning him. Even though such a natural response should be respected, the more mature awareness of an adult, who can understand that the mother did not choose to die and abandon her child, needs to be included. Only then can a person heal the loss and open to his mother and still receive her as an important resource. Otherwise, he remains stuck in a childish reaction, unable to grow up and learn to find elsewhere the love and care that he was not able to get from his mother.

Family Constellation is a very helpful tool for healing such bonding traumas and providing a resource in helping us to connect with primary caregivers. With this connection, co-regulation of an activated physiological trauma state becomes easier.

Combining a somatic view with Family Constellation

Here are a few simple suggestions for integrating Family Constellation and working with the body in a single session, which is especially helpful when dealing with trauma. Lowering arousal and helping the body to discharge before an actual constellation begins can support a client to be more grounded and present. This can help him to be more available to observe and receive the actual constellation, so he can benefit much more from the work and any overwhelm or dissociation can be avoided. Traumatised clients tend to be either hyperactive or in a trance like absence or dissociation, and then a constellation can easily bypass their awareness and the intended healing effect is missed.

Lowering the physical arousal can happen through working with the body without entering the trauma content. One way that we discussed is resourcing, which usually leads to a discharge. Discharge can be observed, for example, when a client gives a deep sigh, when the body goes through some involuntary movements like shaking or trembling, or when the client slows down and contacts some deep feelings like sadness or fear. Another method to lower arousal is to help a person to slightly move his body or extend the area where arousal is experienced, thus making the arousal more tolerable. This will also reduce the need to dissociate.

High activation is usually easier to detect. A client may speak fast without allowing for gaps, he may be physically restless, or the body may show signs of over activation, like fast breathing, reddening of the face or tension in the extremities. Dissociation is less easy to detect and can sometimes be misunderstood. A client might appear to be relaxed, while in reality the high arousal is hidden. It is really only a question of whether the sympathetic or the parasympathetic activation is dominant, but in both situations lowering the arousal can be helpful.

It is usually a much better approach to work on lowering the arousal than to ask a person to be more present or try to help him be more in touch with his body, as is sometimes done in therapy. What may work with other clients may be counterproductive if a client is in a trauma state because the reason why someone dissociates from the body is his inability to handle the high arousal that is trapped inside the body. Simply asking him to connect to his body can create pressure and can lead to further disintegration. However, when the arousal is lowered, then coming back to the body and sensing it will happen more naturally and effortlessly.

Until a client is less charged and also a little less identified with his 'issue', it can be difficult or even impossible to examine any systemic cause and take in what a constellation reveals. But after an activation is reduced, starting a constellation or investigating the family history is likely to have a deeper and more positive outcome.

Integration

Not only before, but also after a constellation, working with the body and noticing physical sensations can be helpful and can support the important process of integrating insights into the physiology. The mind can understand very fast, but our body needs time to readjust and reorganise itself. This can be supported when, after a constellation has ended, a client is asked to track the effects of what he observed in his own body. This has more depth and meaning than just asking a client if he understood, or if everything is clear. Sometimes clients answer such questions by saying 'Yes', when in fact they are responding more out of fear or shock, or not to appear ignorant rather than out of real understanding.

The body shows a person's truth more than any of his words. Therefore, listening to the signals from the body gives a therapist and even the client himself a more reliable feedback about what is really going on inside, what has been understood, or is only an intellectual idea. Real understanding always includes body, mind and heart as a unity. This is also one reason why too much talking about an issue before, during and after a constellation should be avoided, as talking sometimes connects a person more with the neo-cortex. Of course, this depends on how verbal interaction is used within a session.

The starting point

There is another benefit of doing some body tracking before the start of a constellation that I discovered and found very useful. In constellation work, especially when working only with movements, it is essential to find the right starting point for the session. In other words, a facilitator needs to decide who to place in the constellation, and who from the family system to start with. This might be only one or two individuals, but they have to be the right ones, otherwise the work may go in a different direction and no solution for a specific problem will be found. When one starts with fewer representatives, often the work is more focused, but it is also more important to pick the most significant person from the system. Sometimes this can be decided easily, but in many situations, it may be not so obvious.

Watching Bert Hellinger, the founder of Family Constellation, starting a constellation with only one representative, was quite startling at times because of how he decided to choose that particular representative.

I discovered that guiding a client to move through a few cycles of activation and discharge at the beginning of a session without being too concerned about relating this to any family dynamics, leads one in an easy and natural way to finding the right person with whom to start the constellation. Experimenting with this approach, especially with trauma clients, I always found that the body itself will guide me to what is important and, at some point, it becomes obvious to see with whom from the family system the constellation should begin.

Now I will give an example of how working with the body can be combined with doing constellation work.

Session example

A female client of about 40 years old is quite fearful at the start of her session; her body is trembling and she has difficulty in speaking with a normal tone of voice. Before inquiring about her issue, we start with resourcing and I suggest that she doesn't fight with the trembling feeling, but rather focuses on an area of her body that is less affected and relatively calm. This leads to some discharge of her physical activation and in turn helps her to tolerate the remaining tension more easily. I also invite her to look around and see if she feels that she is in a safe and supportive environment. I reassure her that we have plenty of time and will only proceed at her own pace.

After grounding and resourcing her in this way, she tells me that a memory is arising of her father suffocating her with a pillow when she was about 6 years of age. She remembers that she felt that she was going to die. Without going further into this memory, I remind her that she didn't die and, when she relaxes a little, I ask if she remembers where her mother was at the time, and if there was any support available. She tells me that her mother and other siblings were watching the event and seem to have been paralysed. She remembers the feeling of letting go and not fighting. I inquire if this response was perhaps what saved her and she agrees. I point out this ability of her body to respond with letting go and surrendering as something that saved her life.

After this, her energy slowly starts to expand. Previously, her energy had been pulled back from the periphery of her body and held at the core, with her extremities being under-charged and in a state of near-collapse – a typical fear-oriented physical condition to protect oneself. Now her body position changes and her arms become more charged with energy. When I invite her to carefully track her body sensations, she starts noticing the charge as it enters her arms and hands. As this happens, she makes defensive and protective gestures, especially with her right hand and arm, which appear to be a completion of the defense responses against the attack. It seems that this is exactly what the body originally wanted to do, but realising that she did not have the power to fight her father, she stopped and went into freeze.

After following these movements for a while, she feels more grounded, present and stronger. I explain to her what happens in the body after such a traumatic event and also the difficulty for a child to develop self-trust when a parent is unable to be a safe and reliable support for the child.

Now my client is more stable and more ready to look at the family dynamics that may have led her father to become such a threat to her life. It is clear that unless she is eventually able to resolve this issue with her father, it will be difficult to establish healthy relationships with men. In her life, she tends to keep men at a distance, while at the same time searching for a 'father figure', someone who might give her what she missed from her own father. Allowing her to face her father in a constellation at the very beginning might have been overwhelming for her. Such a confrontation without proper preparation could have led to a strong reaction or traumatised her even more, but now she feels better prepared for it. She agrees to investigate her relationship with her father and I reassure her that we will only go as far as she feels comfortable.

So now we choose representatives for her father and for her (I still did not feel I should place the client herself in the constellation, but allow her to watch from a safe distance). When they face each other, various movements start and at the beginning the father cannot see his daughter as his daughter. The representative for the client starts to look at the ground and we place someone there to represent a dead person. The representative of the client lies down next to her. The father seeing this is very moved, but remains frozen. After placing two more men into the picture, more movements happen and it appears that the men represent the father's own father and grandfather, who seem to have murdered someone in the past, which has remained a hidden family secret. This is confirmed by the client. Now the entanglements become clear: Her father took over a murderous impulse from his grandfather, she identified with the victim and the drama of the past was re-enacted in the present between father and daughter.

After the original players in the drama have come into the picture, we now continue to watch the movements that happen between the murderers and their victim to see if they are ready to meet each other. After observing this for some time, we come back to the present and I ask the representatives for the father and the daughter to face each other again. Now there is more acknowledgment possible and the father is for the first time really able to see his child, and the daughter can take a few steps towards him. At this point, we end the constellation, even though it is still incomplete and we also have not yet examined the relationship with her mother, whose support she missed, but which we leave for another time.

I ask the client what she feels as she watched this constellation. Her activation has eased a lot and she is feeling that she can now relax more with her father and even thinks of visiting him, which was difficult for her before and is something she has not done in years. She also feels more at ease about her present life situation and can allow things to develop slowly without being too desperate and forcing herself into having any steady relationship with a man.

This is a simple example of how somatic trauma work and Family Constellation can be combined in one session to reach to a more comprehensive picture. The initial resourcing helped the client to come out from dissociation, freeze and feeling overwhelmed and connected her to her original defense response. After allowing her body to complete this and also explaining to her what happens in trauma and what her body is trying to do, she became more grounded, stable and capable of investigating why her father behaved in such an aggressive way.

When we prematurely try to understand the behaviour of our parents through a constellation, we sometimes easily override our own needs without even acknowledging them. This can create further alienation from our body and can hamper further growth. This danger is reduced when we include somatic bodywork in our session. Love and respect for oneself and understanding our parents (or someone else) should go hand in hand.

Active meditation

Another way to introduce the somatic aspect in constellation work is to combine it with active meditations that involve sensing and moving our body. Active meditations have been especially developed by Osho and include an active, sometimes cathartic and expressive stage, followed by more silent and quiet stages. In this way, watchfulness – which is the essential element in meditation – is not only to be done while being physically inactive, but also while moving the body and being expressive. This helps one to stay in contact with the body and its physical sensations, which can lead to the discovery of repressed emotions and past memories that have been stored in the unconscious part of our mind. In this way, one can avoid the trap of using meditation as a way to escape from unpleasant feelings and sensations, which is a common strategy of some people who practice meditation and use it to by-pass the darker side of their personality. We will discuss this more in Chapter Ten.

In all my workshops and trainings, active meditations are an integral part of the work and they play an important role in grounding people in the physical realm of their being and at the same time helping them to reach their witnessing consciousness, which is beyond body and mind.

It is common that during a constellation a person discovers love and respect for a parent, but when joining the active meditations, another wave of anger and frustration can start to reappear, which shows that more processing and deeper understanding are still needed. Without these meditations, there is the danger that one can stay on the intellectual level and develop illusions about what one has really achieved. All authentic inner growth depends on how we are connected to our body.

Chapter Nine

Love and Relationship

To love oneself, to feel loved and to have fulfilling relationships and friendships is one of the greatest protections against trauma and certainly one of the greatest resources for healing trauma. In this chapter, we will discuss a few considerations about the nature of love and relationship.

Loving oneself

Self-love is the foundation of all love, but this is not taught by any society or any religion. Instead, it is often condemned as egotism. But unless a person can love himself, he is unable to love anybody else. Every child is born with the intrinsic ability to love himself; he is naturally in harmony with his body, his impulses and needs, but gradually gets distracted from himself. He learns that he should love others, above all his parents and family, and whenever he loves himself and follows his own impulses, he often feels rejected. Slowly, he learns ideals about how he should be that are in conflict with his own isness. His joyful harmony with himself and his sense of being one whole is lost.

If a child's love for himself is supported and appreciated, he will develop into a strong and healthy human being, who is joyful and self-confident. Out of this joy, loving others will follow naturally, not because it is taught as a duty or obligation. Also, a joyful person who loves himself, will be loved by other people and this will further strengthen his sense of self-worth. On the other hand, if a person cannot feel any love for himself and constantly seeks to be loved by others in order to fill his own inner emptiness, this neediness tends to repulse others and the feeling of being rejected and the need to be loved increases even more. For many, the only one way out of this negative cycle is to pretend. People pretend to love others, when in reality they desperately need to be loved. This is not personal: it is the consequence of a wrong upbringing from the very beginning.

We need to unlearn and let go of wrong ideals and moral concepts and connect with our natural self again. We need to start listening to the voice of nature within and come into harmony with our body and its impulses. We need to fall in tune with our hearts rather than being driven by mental thought forms about how we should be. Only then can loving oneself become easy and effortless.

Using the word *love*

Even though love is certainly the most important ingredient in all forms of healing, including trauma healing, the word is rarely used in psychological literature. One can read about *connection, co-regulation, bonding or non-duality*, which are more technical terms, but there seems to be some uneasiness about using the word *love*. Maybe it sounds too unscientific or maybe we are all aware of how misused the word *love* is and how difficult it is to understand its real meaning. Language is useful for describing objects, but love is not an object. People talk about loving their car or loving ice cream, just as they say they love their partner or they love to do certain things, not really aware of what they are saying. Love is maybe the most misunderstood and misused word in any language.

One reason might be that there is usually a lot of conditioning about love from an early age. Children are taught to love their parents, their elders, their teachers, as if love is an act that one can perform. We are continuously told how to love, whom to love and when to love, and the simple fact that authentic love cannot be produced to order is forgotten. Love often seems to have become a desire, an expectation – part of the world of doing; we even use it when we try to manipulate others.

So, it becomes difficult to figure out what someone really means, when he or she speaks about love. It could indicate possessiveness, demand, fear of being alone, sexual lust or many other states that are quite contrary to real love. Strangely enough, it is not the same with negative words like anger or hate. No one has taught us how to hate, which may be the reason why hate remains pure, clean and uncorrupted. If someone says: "I hate you", you can be quite sure what he means! The word hate retains an authenticity that the word love does not have.

Nevertheless, love is the most important experience in life and also the most important resource when it comes to healing trauma. But in order to understand its meaning, one needs to first get rid of all the wrong connotations that have become associated with the word love. It is one of the aims of spiritual therapy to investigate and drop these false beliefs and empty oneself of conditioned ideas. Then it becomes possible to discover the authentic love that is at the center of every human being.

Bonding love

Love is a basic need from the very beginning. Love is the nourishment for the soul and just as our body needs food, our soul needs love. It has been shown in scientific studies that primates who have been provided with food, whose physical needs have been fulfilled but have received no loving care, do not grow into healthy adults. Some do not even survive.

In order to ensure that both physical and emotional care will be given to a newborn child, nature creates a strong bond between him and his primary caregiver, usually his parents. We discussed this in detail in Chapter Four. Bonding refers to the process of forming an attachment between parent and child and this is usually strongest between mother and child. There are factors that support the establishment of these healthy bonds, for example breastfeeding, and there are factors that can disturb or even rupture them, for example an early separation between mother and child.

Bonding love always has a strong biological component and gives humans and all mammals a survival advantage over more primitive species. For example, it is generally understood that the production and maternal circulation of the hormone oxytocin predisposes mammals to show care giving behaviour in response to their young ones. The ability to bond helps mammals and also humans to regulate physiological activation in their bodies better and therefore become less prone to being overwhelmed by challenging life experiences. This is also called *co-regulation* and can take place on a physiological as well as on an emotional level and refers to the responsive interaction that provides the support to modulate sensations, feelings, thoughts and behaviour. Co-regulation is especially important for small children, who need a caretaker to help them process experiences that otherwise could easily overwhelm them. An upset or hurt child will run to his mother in order be held by her and in this way the more developed nervous system of the mother will support the undeveloped nervous system of the child to down-regulate its activation and gradually the child will begin to calm down. When bonding is disturbed or fragmented, for example as a consequence of trauma, co-regulation cannot take place properly and some experiences cannot be fully processed. This can disturb the ability to relate to others and can also disturb the relationship to oneself, including one's own body.

Bonding not only helps the individual to process personal experiences, but it also helps larger social groups to process collective experiences and ensures their survival when facing threatening or hostile environments, for example. It can be observed that members of smaller religious groups, cultures or countries develop especially strong bonds with one another in order to ensure that they are not eradicated or overtaken by a larger surrounding majority.

When bonding fails and co-regulation is impossible, the individual retreats to more primitive survival and defence mechanisms like fight and flight. This can be observed in individuals as well as in social groups. In other words, when facing danger, the first natural response is to look for social contact and support, to connect with another human being in order to calm one's activation, and only if this fails – maybe because no one else is available or we have lost the ability to bond because of earlier unresolved trauma – do we resort to the next line of defence, which is fight or flight.

If this is not possible either, maybe because of the nature of the threat, then the last line of defence is to freeze or shut down. This mechanism also exists in more primitive species of animals that do not form social networks.

Sharing love

The biological programme and ability to create bonds and attachments to others has a life-sustaining function and is probably the outcome of millions of years of evolution. At the same time, it fixates us to the level of survival and sometimes prevents us from experiencing higher forms of love, which are not biologically determined and arise only through growing consciousness. When survival needs are fulfilled, we naturally discover other needs that relate to higher brain centers; we feel the need to develop our potential as human beings and our own inner gifts and potential. Now the need to share arises.

Bonding, originally, is survival oriented; it is rooted in a deep need to be safe and secure. When this primal need is satisfied in children, they become interested in exploring their environment, they seek adventure and discover the joy of exploration. A need to expand and grow beyond oneself develops; just being safe is no longer enough. Unless a human being is also adventurous and ready to explore, which is also one of the roots of creativity, he is not growing into this other dimension of love.

The longing to interact with our environment and with others takes us beyond the need to be safe and helps us to develop our potential as human beings. It is also at the root of all spiritual search. Now it becomes less important to be safe, but more important to discover and enjoy sharing. In this space, the fulfilment of love is not in getting something from someone, but in being received and being allowed to share. We still have needs that we want fulfilled, but now a sense of gratitude arises.

In the enlightened vision of Osho, the real uplifting experience is not only receiving, but sharing love. When we demand to be loved, we behave like a beggar, while in sharing love we rise to the status of an emperor.

Being love

Sharing love takes us beyond our biological needs to the level of the heart and when we enter the space of the heart, we can discover that love really does not come from outside, but arises from within. In *bonding love* and *sharing love* we need another person to find fulfilment. In *being love*, we are all alone, complete in ourselves. It is a state of compassion, where love is not a relationship anymore. Now it is possible to experience love not as coming from or being directed towards another person, but as welling up from deep inside one's own heart. This is a love that has grown beyond need and entered a state of being, where fulfilment does not depend on anybody else. The fulfilment is not in getting what we want, but in having no desire and that is the ultimate gift that love can present to us. This may be the reason why mystics have always said that love is a kind of death – a death to our ego and personality.

Even though this kind of love is only reached by people who have arrived at a high state of consciousness, we can sometimes have glimpses of it in special moments, when we experience love as an unaddressed energy coming from deep inside.

It could be said that when one level of love is fully satisfied and complete, the next level becomes available. When bonding has successfully happened and has fulfilled its purpose, then one can move beyond it. In Family Constellation, we learn to acknowledge our early life bonds and develop a more conscious love that is not biologically driven and can take us to another level of love that is beyond bonding. Then the sharing love that we experience in a relationship can take us to a space where we can discover being love, which is not a relationship anymore.

Disconnected from love

In what way does all this relate to trauma?

Trauma is an experience that can disconnect us from experiencing love; it separates us not only from others, but also from ourselves. When someone is in a trauma state, it may be difficult to connect with anybody else; one may not even want to look at another person. One may have difficulty in sensing one's own body or body parts, or accessing feelings as we have discussed in the chapter on dissociation. One often feels lost, disoriented, feeling as if nothing seems to make sense anymore.

In my own experience, it was a feeling as if the whole world had suddenly stopped and my life had come to a halt. I lost the motivation to do anything, except wanting to take care of my wife's art and work. However, I was still feeling the love and care that arrived from so many people from around the world. So, in that way, my connection to others was not fully broken.

Love is the bridge that connects us to others and to everything that surrounds us. If that bridge is broken, a person may experience a deep emptiness and disconnection that can be very difficult to cope with. He may want to reach out to others, but cannot do so. Physiologically, he is dominated by the brain's more primitive defence or survival mechanism and the ability to socially engage is blocked.

Our reaction to stress is hierarchically organised by the autonomous nervous system. When we feel safe and when the vagus nerve is activated, we feel calm and enter a state of relaxation that enables us to make contact with others. This social engagement enhances our sense of safety and creates a positive feedback loop that leads to further calming. When, however, we do not feel safe and our body detects danger, we often switch to the more primitive fight/flight response and then it becomes difficult to operate through the social engagement system. This can lead to a negative feedback loop, where fear leads to further activation until the fight/flight system fails and we resort to the primordial response strategy of freeze and total shutdown.

When danger is detected in a healthy system, it does not immediately need to switch to the fight/flight response, but by staying connected to the social engagement system, in other words by still being able to relate, the activation level can be down-regulated before it moves out of control.

In reality, it is not that a person does not want to connect, but he literally cannot when he is under the influence of the fight/flight system or in total shutdown. Trying to make contact with a person in that state is like talking to a wall. Not only that, but it might be viewed by him as a subtle pressure, which can create further activation or increase the shutdown. Therefore, a better therapeutic strategy is to first induce a calm behavioural state and only then can the social engagement system come back online.

I was very aware for many months after my traumatic experience how I needed to be alone and in a quiet space and how too much social interaction could become intolerable for me. During some meetings with friends, I sometimes had to just get up and leave and be alone; it was as if my body sent me clear signals about what was too much. It was so strong that I could not ignore such impulses. I also was very sensitive about whose support and love I wanted to receive and with whom I wanted to have contact.

Love as a resource

Love is one of the greatest resources we have, but only if it is authentic and not just a superficial niceness or politeness. Our social conditioning often confuses us into believing that being nice means to be loving, because children are frequently taught to be nice, rather than to be honest and truthful. In reality, an honest response is always loving, while a dishonest response is not.

When a child grows up in an atmosphere of love,

where his bonding needs are met, he develops into a healthy and resilient human being. Authentic love makes a person strong and creates confidence, courage and a sense of self-worth. He becomes ready to explore the world around him and to discover his own unique creative expression. Moreover, he will be more capable of dealing with life's challenges and is less prone to be traumatised. Not feeling loved on the other hand makes a person insecure, doubtful, hesitant, fearful and self-critical and more susceptible to trauma.

In my experience, love helped me to deal with the loss of my wife and carry on with my life. It was the love that I received from others while I was on my own in South Africa, my friend who was ready to travel to South Africa to support me and all the people who sent me messages. For many weeks, some close friends would be available to talk to me on the phone and I could share my feelings of agony with them.

But it was not only that; it was also the love that I felt coming from my wife when I tuned into her. I always felt how she was concerned about me and was trying to let me know that she was in a beautiful space. Even though sometimes my mind would interfere and tell me that this was all my imagination, I somehow trusted it, because I could still feel her energy around. Also, my love for her kept me going and the determination I felt to take care of her art and the continuation and expansion of the work that she had created over decades. I felt strongly that I owed this to her, and this seemed the only important thing left for me to do in this life.

It is important in trauma therapy to investigate the social field a person is living in and whether he has enough social contacts and whether there are people who can love and support him. A traumatised person is often not easily reachable for social contact when he is under the influence of the fight/flight system. It can therefore be a delicate matter for his social environment to know when to offer support, while at the same time tolerating his impulse to withdraw or even react aggressively. Sometimes only professional help can ease the pressure that is placed upon a person's relationships after a traumatic event. The need to be close to someone can suddenly turn into a violent rejection, which is not easy for close friends or family members to understand and it can provoke reactions in them that may cause him to withdraw further. It can be a long process to relearn how to regulate one's own energies after a traumatic event.

Only individuals who themselves are well regulated can support someone to find self-regulation again. We are equipped by nature with the ability to regulate each other, physiologically, emotionally and mentally. Most mammals will seek each other's company when facing danger, and in this way can help to regulate each other's activation before having to recede to the more primitive fight/flight response. This co-regulation, where others process a part of our own activation, can help us to calm down. But it can also activate us, for example, when we take on the activation of another person. Depending on which social field we enter, we can either feel calmer and safer or we may feel more fearful and agitated.

Co-regulation is defined as the warm responsive interaction that someone can provide to someone else, in order for the other to modulate his feelings, thoughts and behaviour. This is especially important for children, for their development and in order to learn secure bonding. If this co-regulation is missing and the child's bonding needs are not properly responded to, they develop insecure bonding styles in their way of relating to others. (Review also Chapter Four)

Understanding Relationship

The experience of love can happen within a relationship, or it may not. Love essentially is a state of mind, not a relationship. In a relationship, two individuals, more or less consciously, enter into an agreement, which is why they each have certain expectations of the other. Love, on the other hand, is not an expectation and not an act that can be done. Real love is not in our control and we cannot just decide to love someone – it comes as a gift from the beyond. When we act 'loving', then we will eventually become tired and need to relax, which is the moment when this kind of love turns into its opposite and becomes hate.

In a relationship, two individuals give and take from each other and if love is also present, then this giving and taking is accompanied by a feeling of gratitude towards the other person. Family Constellation differentiates between different kinds of relationships. The parent-child and the man-woman relationships are the two main prototypes: The first is between unequals and the second between equals. In the first, there is imbalance between giving and taking, as parents give more and children receive more. The second, if it is healthy, is balanced, in the sense that giving and taking happen equally from both sides.

With this understanding, it is easy to see when there is a disturbance in any of these relationships. If children try to give to their parents and parents try to receive from their children, the nature of their relationship is disturbed and unhappiness is the consequence. In a man-woman relationship, the disturbance happens when one wants to either give or get more than the other is able or ready to give back. If this happens, then the man woman relationship is turned into a parent-child relationship and as we all know conflict, fight and suffering follow. In my book *The Roots of Love* on Family Constellation I have further expanded on this topic.

As many of us have unresolved issues with our parents, it is very common to project a parent onto a partner and then start expecting to be loved unconditionally, just as we expected this in childhood from our parents. If we develop some awareness about our childhood needs without forgetting the reality of our partner, then occasionally being 'mothered' or 'fathered' by our partner does not have to create problems. We can heal some of our childhood wounds in a present relationship; in fact, every woman also has motherly qualities and every man has fatherly qualities. The problem arises if behaving like a parent or a child in a relationship becomes the predominant style of relating, and relating as adults is reduced to a minimum or completely absent.

To see the reality of a partner is often not easy, as, especially in the beginning of a relationship, we project our unfulfilled childhood dreams on the other. A relationship grows once we see and agree to our partner's limitations. Limitations are usually created by incomplete issues both partners have with their parents and original family, or with a former partner. We tend to act out and repeat old conflicts from the past often with little awareness, and this becomes clear when a couple repeatedly have the same conflicts, which seem insoluble. A constellation can reveal the root cause of those disturbances, which lie in an unresolved past; and this can sometimes involve a few previous generations.

Example from a session

A couple from Turkey has repeated conflicts that occur around similar issues and seem insoluble. Upon investigating their family background, we find that the ancestors of the woman were Turks, who had originally lived in Greece for generations, but had to escape to Turkey during the time of the partition, the war between Greece and Turkey. In the constellation, it is revealed that she carries the anger of her mother and grandmother, who were full of rage towards Greeks, but expresses it towards her husband. His ancestors originally came from a different country too and they both seem to be repeating the violent fights and conflicts that their former family members had to go through. In systemic work, we call this a double shift: She takes over the anger of her mother (shift in the subject) and expresses it not towards those Greeks, but towards her partner, who had nothing to do with the original conflict (shift in the object). By finding a partner whose family is originally also from another country, there is an unconscious intention to heal a past conflict, but at the same time the bonding towards one's own family members does not allow one to come very close to the other. Instead, an old conflict, in this case the ancient conflict between Turks and Greeks, is repeated and played out within the relationship.

Unlike in ordinary therapy, in spiritual therapy the therapist is less concerned with helping a couple to stay together, but instead investigates what is best for each individual's personal development. It could be the case that a separation is better for someone's personal growth, or that staying together and passing through a conflict helps another to mature. At the beginning of a session, this is not clear and there should be no fixed goal or preference on the part of the therapist. In order to be unprejudiced, a therapist needs to be aware of any hidden values he may carry, and of any hidden conscience that might influence his mind and not allow him to observe clearly. Spiritual therapy is concerned with awareness, not with moral or social values.

Spiritual therapy will help a client to be aware and agree to the fact that all relationships, even those which last a very long time, are going to end at some point. Everything else is a dream that keeps one in unconsciousness. Conscious love on the other hand does not need to end, as love has no boundaries and no limitations. It can go on growing and expanding endlessly; it is not confined to the material and physical plane. It is therefore very significant to differentiate between love and relationship, and to grow beyond bonding love.

From this point of view, bonding love is not really love at all, as it is concerned with safety and security, and is therefore fear oriented, which is quite the opposite of real love. Being identified with our body and mind, which are temporary phenomena that will eventually disappear, will always keep us in fear and misery. Only a meditative consciousness can have a taste of the timeless and of higher dimensions of love. Relationships can be understood as lessons where we learn about this love that is rooted in meditation.

Meditation

Sit comfortably and close your eyes. Look at your life as if you are looking at a movie, where everything changes every moment. Remember when you were young – your body looked very different, you had different friends and you lived in a different place. Since then, everything has been continuously changing. Your body has changed, your friends and lovers have changed. Many people have disappeared from your life and many people have appeared. Nothing has remained the same and nothing will ever remain the same. One day, you will be old and one day you will die and nothing of your body or mind will remain. Eventually, you will be forgotten.

Now become aware of that which does not change in you, which eternally will be the same. There is a witnessing consciousness that continuously observes and watches. This witness never changes; it does not get old or sick and it does not die. Right now, there is someone watching. At the periphery, everything changes, whereas at the center, everything remains the same. Love on the periphery is always changing, coming and going. Love at your center is always there, never lost.

(This meditation is inspired by the meditation 'Be the Unsame Same' from Vigyan Bhairav Tantra)

Chapter Ten

The Role of Meditation

The ability to disidentify with body and mind is another important resource for healing trauma. Trauma can only happen to our body or mind, not to our inner essence. The practice of meditation and mindfulness strengthens our sense of being a witness rather than just a body or mind.

Dissociation is not meditation

In this context, it is important to distinguish between a dissociated state and a meditative state of mind. Dissociation can also give us a feeling of not being affected by what happens to our body or in our mind and we may feel like a distant observer. The important difference to a meditative state is that in meditation one is still sensing the body, one is still in contact with feelings, while in dissociation one disconnects from either the body or from one's feelings, or from other elements of reality.

It can sometimes be difficult to decide if a person, who claims to be relaxed or in a state of witnessing when facing challenging life events, is actually dissociated or has really achieved a certain centering, where such events do not disturb or overwhelm him. As both states can appear similar when observed from the outside, an onlooker can only distinguish between each of these states by relying on his own awareness or inner sense of presence. If one can feel a deepening of one's own meditative quality or an inner expansion, then this can indicate that the person who claims to be a witness is really in a meditative state of presence rather than just dissociated.

Dissociation can sometimes be the only possible way to cope with a difficult or traumatic situation, as we discussed in Chapter Two. It is an important coping mechanism and should therefore not be judged as wrong. But it is also essential that it be recognised for what it is, rather than trying to overcome it too quickly or mistaking it for a developed state of consciousness. We gain strength and awareness when we become capable of returning from a dissociated state and processing the unpleasant or overwhelming feelings that led to dissociation in the first place. Inner growth happens when we fully face reality as it is, including unwanted feelings and sensations.

Spiritual bypassing

Spiritual bypassing, a term introduced by John Welwood, a Buddhist teacher and psychotherapist, should be mentioned in this context. It is defined as a "tendency to use spiritual ideas and practices to sidestep or avoid facing unresolved emotional issues, psychological wounds, and unfinished developmental tasks"[3]

People sometimes hide their true feelings behind spiritual practices or concepts and pretend that everything is all right when it is clearly not. This can serve as a defence mechanism against unwanted feelings, like anger for example, or other feelings that

---

[3] Fossella, Tina; Welwood, John (2011). Human nature, buddha nature: an interview with John Welwood.

are too painful to deal with. One may hide personal insecurity behind a belief in spiritual superiority, or avoid taking responsibility for one's own actions by saying: *It was meant to happen* or *there is a deeper meaning behind it all*. Rather than processing a traumatic event and dealing with panic and sadness, one may dismiss one's own or other people's feelings as just *a learning experience*. The valuable effect of meditation and spiritual practice is then used to pretend to oneself or to others to be spiritually superior.

Spiritual bypassing therefore creates barriers to authentic personal growth. One can avoid falling into the trap of spiritual bypassing by staying connected to common sense and by remaining grounded in ordinary life activities, doing them with awareness, rather than seeking special spiritual experiences. It is also important not to label emotional states as good or bad, but be prepared to deal with anything that appears uncomfortable or difficult, or that shatters old beliefs.

We often have a tendency to adhere to concepts and theories that support our own set beliefs and then dismiss anything that could disturb what we already believe to be true. The worldwide controversy during the recent coronavirus crisis is a perfect example, demonstrating how our mind is unable to tolerate 'cognitive dissonance' and only wants to take in information that supports our existing set of beliefs.

Meditative practice can be a great resource in healing trauma, but it can also be used to bypass dealing with trauma and then it stifles personal growth.

Active Meditation - Roots in the body

It is helpful to start a meditative practice by including the body rather than by sitting silently or only doing Vipassana meditation. The reason is that the modern man is so full of tension and repressions that just by sitting he may not be able to come to a state of witnessing, but is more likely to be flooded with repressed emotions and thoughts that do not allow him to stay present and alert, but are more likely to create sleepiness, restlessness or daydreaming.

Body and mind are one and once we learn to unload from our body the physical tensions that often correspond to repressed emotions, our mind will be less loaded with thoughts, worries and anxieties, which will make witnessing easier. Maybe this is one of the reasons why Osho created many different active meditations, especially for the modern man, where one first passes through a cathartic stage before entering into stillness. The most famous of these meditations are Osho Dynamic and Osho Kundalini meditations, which include different stages of body movements, dance and staying still, while practicing watchful alertness (Detailed instructions can be found on www.osho.com).

Active meditation seems to be a contradiction in terms because meditation is about witnessing, relaxation and non-doing. However, active meditation means going to the very extreme of doing and using one's total energy. This seems to be paradoxical and could be compared to what is called a *koan* in the East.

A *koan* is a riddle that a Zen Master gives to his disciples, which has no apparent solution. By trying to find an answer and meditating on the koan day in day out, the disciple finally comes to a point where the mind stops: and in fact, this is the real answer.

Active meditation is something similar. One has to do two opposite things at the same time, making all possible effort and at the same time staying absolutely relaxed. If you only make an effort and force yourself, nothing seems to happen, and it's the same if you avoid effort from the very beginning. Active meditation is the art of effortless effort, of doing and non-doing both together, which is something our mind cannot grasp. It cannot be explained, but only experienced and has to be discovered by entering into it. A real let-go only happens after one has tried everything possible and understands the futility of all effort.

There is another reason why body-oriented meditation can be helpful. Mind activity cannot be stopped voluntarily and our thoughts can be compared to a radio that has no off switch. The more one tries to be silent, the more noise is created. And this mental activity needs energy, which we usually provide by giving attention to our thoughts. When, however, we spend our energy in physical activity, there is less energy available for mental activity. It is easy to observe that after strenuous physical activity the mind is usually more silent and there are less thoughts passing through our heads. In such moments, becoming a witness of those thoughts is much easier than when our mind is crowded by all kinds of memories, desires, images, fantasies and ideas. This is one of the reasons why athletes or people who do hard physical labour often have a more silent mind.

Are active meditations retraumatising?

There is a common prejudice among trauma therapists and their clients that active or cathartic meditations are dangerous, as they can retraumatise a client. In other words, a client can again be flooded by overwhelming feelings that he cannot control and this can make his symptoms or situation worse – something we want to avoid in trauma therapy, as discussed in Chapter Six.

Even though this can be a real issue that needs to be considered with particular clients, in my view it also depends on how active meditation is introduced and in what way a person practices it. The focus in meditation should not be on any release or on getting rid of anything, but on watchfulness. The moment we have a goal or an idea about what we want to achieve, we are no longer a witness and we have lost the meditative attitude. Meditation is about being fully in the present moment without thinking about the next or the previous moment. Connecting to our body will support this attitude, as becoming aware of body sensations will automatically bring us into the Here and Now.

Sometimes for a severely traumatised person sensing the body can be overwhelming, just as contacting strong emotions can be frightening. This is the reason why one should enter into it gradually and the focus should be on witnessing. In certain situations, and for certain clients it is clearly not advisable to join a cathartic meditation, because the focus may need to be more on calming their system and finding some equilibrium. On the other hand, it is also not helpful to have a more or less subtle attitude of worrying or being apprehensive about the possibility of becoming retraumatised. This also can fixate a person in a fear-oriented trauma state instead of supporting him to rediscover his own strength and independence. I have seen various trauma therapists and their clients who seem to be so fearful of anything that could be retraumatising, like an active meditation, that the client is not allowed to test his capacity to deal with life's challenges.

Beyond body and mind

In my view, it is essential to learn a meditative or mindfulness practice during any type of healing approach, because from a spiritual perspective we are all ill, in the sense that we are identified with our body and mind. It is only the degree of our illness that may differ. The existential fact is that both body and mind are going to disappear one day and when we stay identified with our body or our personality, we cannot move beyond fear. In other words, fear is part of the body and the mind and belongs to its biological programme to keep us alive as long as possible. In this sense, fear has a life sustaining function. However, there is an obvious limit to this function, as anything material is bound by the law of change.

Death can actually happen at any moment and the mind's intention to create safety and comfort can never be fully achieved; safety is always relative and always momentary. Only by knowing a reality that is beyond body and mind can we experience ourselves as part of this existence and have a taste of a space beyond fear, where there is always safety and security. For an enlightened mystic, this is an experience, while for most of us it is just a beautiful idea. Meditation can bring us closer to experiencing this space.

From the mystic's perspective, life has two dimensions – one of change and one of eternity. On the periphery, everything always changes and it does not matter whether an experience is pleasant or unpleasant, it will change anyway into its opposite. That's why Eastern mystics have described life as an eternal drama and likened it to a dream, not in the sense of being unreal, but in the sense of being an ever-changing flux. At the center, in our innermost core, nothing ever changes, the witness is always the same, never gets sick or old and cannot die. But we are all identified with the outside; we live on the periphery and are usually oblivious of our inner center. When one discovers this center, one is not dissociated, but disidentified.

Meditation: Dying consciously

Lie down on your back and imagine you have died and you cannot move your body. Your body has suddenly become dead and you cannot move your eyes or any other part of your body. You cannot cry or do anything at all. Observe how this feels.

Notice any feelings that come to you, maybe anxiety or anger or sorrow, but remember that you are dead and cannot do anything. Just stay as you are without doing anything at all, not even the slightest movement. Remember that your body has died.

Now look at your life as if it is a dream. The body is like an empty shell and you see your whole life just as if you are watching a long dream. Everything is a dream and you are also a dream. Whether the dream is beautiful or a nightmare, it is all the same dream.

After some time allow your body to move again and come slowly back.

(This meditation is taken from the book *Vigyan Bhairav Tantra, Vol I, #9a*)

My experience

After Meera's accident, I had a feeling of being in a trance or in a nightmare. It felt as if someone had hit a huge bell and I was enveloped by the vibrating sound. I had a feeling as if, at any moment, I would wake up from this nightmare and then everything would be over. My mind was continuously saying, 'Why don't I wake up?' The whole world around me appeared unreal, like a surreal movie. Nothing seemed to have any importance anymore, only Meera's body that was lying in my lap. I just wanted to go with her. Waves of strong guilt went through me that I had not taken care of her, as if I had killed my beloved.

I lost the sense of time and did not know how long I sat with Meera's body or how much time had passed. A few hours seemed like days. Without the need to take care of practical matters, I would have preferred to just sit and sit forever and disappear in this way. I had the experience of being out of my personality, as if my mind and body were separate from me. In all my agony, this was almost blissful. Then I had these strong guilt attacks. My whole life had stopped and nothing made any sense anymore.

I also had my own cathartic release, which in retrospect, I would say, helped me not to develop any lasting symptoms of post-traumatic stress. A few times I had emotional outbursts, once when driving behind the caretaker's car, where I just screamed and screamed, and one time after hearing the news that Meera's air cylinder had been closed. On hearing this, I almost fainted. I could barely stand up. I went to my hotel room, sent my friend out and screamed and beat some cushions for quite a while. I felt as if my beloved had been killed.

On one hand, I was dissociated from my body and my feelings and that allowed me to still take care of practical matters. On the other hand, I was so awake with the adrenalin that must have been in my blood stream that I hardly slept for a whole week. I also assume that my own practice of having learned to be watchful of the mind helped me to stay sane, and some glimpses that we are not just our body helped me not to become completely overwhelmed by what was happening.

Trauma and awakening

Trauma has the potential to awaken us from our dreaming state of consciousness and come out of our identification with our personality. Trauma is a shock, just like an alarm clock that can wake us up. It may be an accident, a serious illness or the sudden loss of a loved one that interrupts our routine life – and nothing is the same anymore. This can be very painful and a huge shock. At the same time, it can interrupt our sleep and unconscious state of being. This may be one reason why it is said that trauma is one of the doorways to higher consciousness.

Enlightened mystics have always stated that man as he is, is asleep and dreaming. At night, he dreams with closed eyes and in the day with open eyes, but as long as layers of thoughts cloud one's present moment awareness, one cannot be really called awake. Only when thoughts cease and the mind is silent one can be called awake. A traumatic event can make one's mind stop, at least for a moment.

I was completely unprepared for Meera's accident and did not pay attention to the small signs that something was not okay. My mind was somewhere in the future, thinking and preparing for the dive. After the accident, my mind was running like mad in endless and useless circles, repeating the same memories, asking constantly, 'What if...'. But besides this, I also had moments of absolute stillness, as if everything had suddenly come to a halt – nothing made sense anymore and the mind had nothing to do. Future and past were no longer important; my life had stopped and with it my mind stopped too.

In trauma, the mind stops in its routine, something happens that is not in its control. For example, in an accident, one cannot do anything and the mind stops. It is not trained or prepared for what is happening and therefore cannot function. Unless one starts again doing something for which one is trained, the mind goes blank and one is thrown to one's center. This can become a moment of meditation.

Even though taking care of Meera's art was a help to me to carry on, I sometimes felt that I missed an opportunity of being more fully in the gap, because the mind found something else to do. As far as the situation was concerned, I could not do anything, I could only be aware.

Usually, we are never fully in the Here and Now, as our mind is constantly thinking about past or future, planning what we will do next and therefore not fully experiencing the present moment. If we happen to be more present, it is usually because something has taken us by surprise. Some unexpected event made our mind stop and this is more so if this event is painful, or even traumatic. Many times, people change their life path and turn towards meditation after having been told they have a serious illness, after losing a loved one, or after having experienced a personal blow or disaster. Suddenly, they wake up to what is really meaningful for them and they may re-evaluate their life or find some new direction. Now the old defences, rationalisations and postponements seem meaningless.

Trauma teacher Peter Levine describes it like this:

"The 'awe-ful' states of horror and terror appear to be connected to the transformative states such as awe, presence, timelessness, and ecstasy. ...Trauma sufferers, in their healing journeys, learn to dissolve their rigid defences. In healing the divided self from its habitual mode of disassociation, they move from fragmentation to wholeness. In becoming embodied, they return from their long exile. ...The survival response embedded within trauma can also catalyse authentic spiritual transformation." (In an Unspoken Voice by Peter Levine, North Atlantic Books 2010)

An authentic spiritual experience is not about being blissful, but about being able to hold a space for both bliss and agony. It is the ability to allow expansion and contraction simultaneously, without being attached to what seems pleasant and trying to avoid what is unpleasant and painful. When one moves towards the center of pain, one also reaches the center of bliss, and vice versa.

Witnessing is not really an act, not anything one can do, but happens when one can stay in 'neutral gear', not seeking bliss or avoiding pain, but just being with what is.

For months after the accident, I had these sudden pain attacks. It could happen anywhere and I was overtaken by a wave of sadness and deep pain, with tears rolling down my face. Most of the time, I didn't bother about others or the situation I was in, but just allowed myself to be with it. It was usually an intense moment and soon it subsided and it always left me feeling relieved.

Trauma has the potential to awaken us from our spiritual sleep and make us realise that we are not just a body or a mind. At the same time, having practiced meditation and watchfulness can help us to overcome or better deal with any aftereffects of a traumatic experience.

When trauma disturbs or destroys our identification or attachments to a person or to what we want to do in life, the energy that went into these desires is suddenly freed. Now this energy is not moving anywhere, but just sitting at the center and we are at home.

Chapter Eleven

Creativity as a Healing Factor

Generally, in therapy, we try to complete unresolved issues and traumas of the past. This can happen either psychologically, as in the approach of Family Constellation, or more physiologically, for example when we help our body to process stuck or frozen energy. Trauma symptoms can be understood as the expression of an incomplete and unprocessed defence reaction that was originally supposed to last for a short time, but has become entrenched in the body. Imagine an old vinyl record that has a deep scratch and continuously plays the same phrase over and over again, without being able to move forward. A therapist will usually examine what it is in his client's past that needs completion or re-evaluation and by supporting him to do this can help him to move on and be more fully available to the present moment.

There is another way that can help a person to overcome a fixation in the past and that is to find his inner motivation and true passion for what he would like to do in life. When we are more in touch with our deeper self and discover how our unique individuality wants to express itself creatively, we become less focused on past events, and instead find a joy that arises out of coming closer to truly being ourselves. We then sometimes develop a clear vision for the future that is not a dream or desire, but which arises from a meditative consciousness and a rootedness in the Here and Now. We discussed this in the previous chapter, but now I want to emphasise the additional element of creativity.

Meditation alone can be passive, while authentic creativity is alive, and full of joy, as if an old tree is bursting into new blossom.

When we are in touch with our genuine creative expression, it becomes easier to cope with a traumatic experience in the past. Creative expression can be used to heal trauma and rediscover one's lost self–regulation. Of course, it is also true that trauma can hinder a person's creative self-expression and become a barrier to finding self-connection. It works both ways, which is why it can be very effective to combine therapy and creativity in one single approach, just as therapy and meditation should also go hand in hand. Therapy helps us to overcome a traumatic fixation in the past and creativity allows us to find the meaning and motivation to move forward in life.

Surge in creativity after trauma

Many famous artists had a traumatic childhood and many creative people have found creative inspiration by struggling with the traumas they suffered in the past. In such moments, old ideas, routines and concepts are suddenly broken or become dysfunctional and a person is almost forced to find new meaning or a new direction in life. Often after traumatic events, people move into solitude, and in their aloneness discover a strength or ability they never knew they had. A traumatic experience is deeply individual and cannot be shared with anyone; one feels alone, even when friends are there for support.

Sometimes people change the direction of their life completely in work or relationship, or feel impelled to move on a spiritual path. Not all of these changes are necessarily creative ways of coping, but one certainly needs to find a very personal way of dealing with the experience of trauma and discovering anew what really matters and is meaningful in one's life.

In my own experience, I had never felt so alone ever before in my life, even though I had the support of many people, who showered love on me. Maybe for the first time, I became so conscious of how alone we all are, as it was crystal clear to me that I could not share this experience with anybody. Suddenly, all that I had done before in my life had lost all meaning and significance. It meant nothing anymore and any attachment had just disappeared.

I had to discover anew what to live for and why to continue being here. All concepts and theories about healing and how to overcome trauma were utterly meaningless for me. I only knew one thing: I wanted to take care of Meera's art and support the continuation of her life's work. And that, especially, kept me going. It was now the only remaining attachment.

In the coming months and years, my life changed a lot. I could never have imagined that I would ever create a foundation, hold art exhibitions, create a museum or even conduct art courses. My life took a completely new turn that I could never have dreamt of.

Certainly, over time, my old habits and patterns came back, but deep inside I cannot be so identified anymore with what I do or want.

Resilience and post-traumatic growth

Resilience is the ability to recover or bounce back from adversities or difficult life events. This can refer to the emotional, physical, mental or spiritual level.

Post-traumatic growth is the positive psychological change that occurs as a result of having struggled with life or death experiences. When we feel shaken to our roots, the old foundations of our life may have lost meaning and we are challenged to change ourselves and discover a new direction in life. One key factor that can help to turn adversity in our favour is whether we are still able to connect to a sense of gratitude and a 'yes' to life. Of course, we may still feel desperate about what happened and would choose another direction if that were possible, but if we can still find moments of gratitude for being alive and for having been showered with gifts, then whatever happened may not just shake our very roots, but may eventually bring us a special strength, depth and inner integrity. This requires that we process rather than avoid dealing with the painful feelings, physical sensations and sometimes unsettling thoughts that come up in the aftermath of a traumatic event.

After Meera's sudden departure, my mind was trying to negotiate with death to offer something so that Meera could stay a little longer. It was a child's mind that wanted to turn the course of events backwards and bargain with death to take a different route. But despite those desperate and torturous moments, there were also moments where I felt a deep serenity and gratitude for having been able to spend so many years at the side of this remarkable woman. It was as if agony and gratitude were just close by, as if side by side and not poles apart. I cannot say exactly how all this influenced my way of coping, but somehow I found the energy to take care of many things and continue Meera's and my work.

After a traumatic event, the mind often goes through endless agonising loops that are repetitive and automatic, but sometimes, when used more deliberately, it can lead to a questioning of old beliefs and mind patterns and eventually help us find a new perspective.

My mind was going through these torturing thoughts, feeling so responsible that I took Meera to that diving trip, which she would never have done on her own. I felt so responsible, as if it was because of me that she left the body, and how much more contribution she would have been able to make to life if I would have taken better care of her. While having these ongoing loops, which sometimes made me want to hit my head against a wall, I also became so sharply aware of how much importance I gave myself and how this feeling responsible was a big part of my ego structure and served as a strategy to try to and control life.

Ultimately, we will find inner strength and grounding only when we develop our ability to be watchful of both mind and body. But this watchfulness should not be a way to avoid dealing with painful feelings. In fact, if there is any intention to avoid, then this kind of watchfulness is not really meditation, but dissociation.

Just as someone's meditation practice can be a form of dissociation, this can also happen with creativity. Some people turn towards creative activities in order not to deal with painful feelings, as in the case of artists who withdraw from reality into their own world, because facing reality is too painful. Dissociation as such is not 'wrong', but should be recognised for what it is and eventually one should slowly begin to deal with past wounds. There is another, more authentic creative expression that does not arise from dissociation, but comes from a deep acceptance and response to life. Out of such a response one may change direction after a traumatic event and discover new insights into one's mind and the source of suffering.

Subjective and objective art

It is difficult to define beauty, as beauty comes from a communion with the heart. Nevertheless, there has been a long philosophical controversy about the nature of beauty, whether it is subjective and solely depends on the onlooker or whether there are objective criteria to define what is beautiful.

Osho and George Gurdjeff distinguish between subjective and objective art. Subjective art is personal and private, an expression of an artist's mind without any consideration of the person who will see the piece of art. This can be therapeutic and helpful for the artist himself and can sometimes work like an inner catharsis, but it may not be of any benefit to an onlooker. Objective art, however, does not arise from the mind, but from a deep meditative inner state. Those who have created objective art, mostly mystics in the east, were concerned with the people watching and how to create in them the same feelings of inner silence and peace that they themselves had experienced.

According to Osho's view, when one looks or listens to objective art, one gains health, wholeness, silence and peace. One is moved to commune with nature and out of such communion religiousness arises. That is the reason why authentically creative people are very close to a meditative experience.

According to the mystic's view, authentic creativity has to come from an inner silence, from emptiness. Osho puts it like this: "Whenever you are creating something, all that has to be remembered is that it is coming out of a silence within you, that it has a spontaneity. It is not prearranged, pre-programmed, pre-thought. As you are creating something, you go on being surprised yourself – you have left yourself in the hands of existence."

From such a perspective, what is often considered to be creativity in society is not authentic creativity, but a by-product of a person's mind or ego. That is why artists sometimes appear more egocentric than ordinary people. This kind of creative expression comes from trying to prove something or be someone special. It is the outcome of desire, not of inner emptiness.

In her courses, Meera helped her students to be aware of this difference and supported them to recognise and nourish moments of spontaneity and emptiness. As this kind of expression has a much bigger healing potential, I will now briefly describe how Meera worked with creative expression in order to illustrate this point.

The development of Osho Art Therapy

Traditional art therapy uses art, for example painting, sculpting, working with clay, singing etc. as a way to heal from traumatic experiences. A client's expression is sometimes analysed and interpreted and the client finds ways through creative expression to heal emotional wounds.

Meera developed this further. In her work, the creative expression is not only used as a therapy with no deeper significance, but is at the same time an in-depth exploration into the nature of creativity. In other words, it is an inquiry into how to find one's own unique creative expression and ultimately into understanding the meaning of objective art, which is born out of meditation. Then painting itself will connect the painter to joy, peace, silence and love.

Meera taught people how to be more alive and spontaneous and follow their inner impulses while painting, not planning what to do or applying a learned technique, but being free from the achieving mind. She used dance, playful exercises and many other therapeutic methods and meditations to lead participants beyond the mind and free them from the psychological blocks of early life conditioning. While painting, she invited participants to be playful with the colours and other equipment, abandoning any idea of the outcome. Authentic creativity is usually born out of playfulness and joy.

Meera created a unique process called 'Primal Painting', where participants learned to connect to this state of innocence while painting and being creative. She called this the foundation and backbone of all her other teachings. Participants would learn to come out of repetitive or routine behaviour patterns and invent themselves anew each moment. For this, Meera invented exercises where one had to learn to be open to being disturbed, for example by other painters, and thus move beyond one's own limitations. It is always our mind that does not like to be disturbed and seeks security and certainty and therefore tends to be repetitive. Creativity, however, is always new, always fresh, always seeks new ways of expression and of doing things.

Meera did not want to teach specific painting techniques, but she preferred to support people in finding their own sensitivity, spontaneity, self-trust and then following their natural flow of energy. In this way, her students learned to paint from their guts, not from the intellect and they learned to be connected to their own originality. They started to create paintings that were not coming from the head, or intellect, but emerged through spontaneous action, playfulness and an awareness of the present moment.

Creativity can be experienced in two ways: Either you can do the same action in a new way, as if for the first time, or you continuously keep changing what you do. This reminds me how Meera was always very excited about her work and returning home after a training, she would say: "This is the best training I ever did!" It never became a routine for her and even when she repeated an exercise, she did it in a new way. Her assistants were often stressed because she changed her ideas of what to do at the last moment and all the preparations had to be changed in a very short time.

Childish or child-like

It will be helpful to mention here the difference between being childish and childlike. When we are childish, we basically regress into being a child; we literally become the child we once were, often forgetting that we may be

40 or 50 years of age. Child-likeness is different. We do not regress, but remain rooted in the Here and Now, yet are able to act from an innocence and spontaneity that is like the action of a child, which appears so beautiful and total. However, the child himself is not aware of this, as he still lives in a state of unconsciousness. A child-like state is a state of awareness that combines the beauty and innocence of a child with the consciousness of an adult.

I want to give an example here from one of our Primal Painting courses to illustrate the difference between being childish and child-like.

After guiding participants to remember a state of child-like innocence in their earlier life and then inviting them to paint from that space, one woman started to paint an animal, with green grass and a blue sky as background. She later described how she remembered that as a child she liked to paint animals, but used to get judged about her way of painting. It was evident that it was important and healing for her to remember herself as a child and support what she enjoyed painting when she was small. However, during the course she started to realise that connecting to the innocence she had as a child didn't mean that she now needed to do what she enjoyed as a child. In fact, painting animals now in the manner of a child, looked childish and was not an authentic and spontaneous expression of who she was now, because she obviously had used her mind and remembered how she painted in childhood. Rather than painting animals in the way she did as a child, she learned to connect to the innocent quality she had as a child and then allow herself to play with colours and water in a spontaneous way without having any idea in the mind of what to paint.

Meera mentioned in her book on art therapy that Picasso in some of his paintings copied the way children would paint. It was not his own authentic expression, but he just copied children's way of painting.

Ultimately to be truly creative, one has to learn not to copy anybody, even a good teacher or an innocent child, but to pick up the essential message or quality and then find and discover one's own and original way of self-expression. Everybody has something unique to contribute to this life that no one else is capable of. In my view, it is one of our tasks to explore and discover what that unique expression is. Only then will we feel an aliveness and deep inner fulfilment and joy. If such inner joy grows in us, we are moving on the right path. Early life conditioning has distracted us from ourselves and planted artificial goals and ambitions in our minds that leave us empty and not in tune with our original nature. It is one of the objectives of Meera's courses to help people rediscover the lost playfulness that they had as a small child.

Session examples

Not being able to find one's true passion or follow a creative impulse can be the result of a wrong upbringing, but can also be caused by an unresolved personal or systemic past trauma. As we can see in Family Constellation, bonding to other members of the family, sometimes from a former generation, can inhibit our creative expression. Superficially, it may appear that being playful and enjoying in a child-like way is easy, but in reality, our unconscious bonds to previous generations, mainly to those who suffered, do not allow us to be so free and undisturbed. Most people talk about wanting to be happy, but their actions have quite the contrary result.

Session 1

A female musician came for a session, feeling unhappy as she had dropped out of her band, had not played for many years and had started to live with her parents again. Her father was also a musician and in her mother's family there was a trauma. Her grandmother, her mother's mother, had lost her own twin at birth.

In the constellation, her mother showed anger and disappointment towards her own mother, who did not appear very available for her daughter and was looking at someone who had died, which seemed to be her sister. The client on the other hand showed love to her grandmother and was trying to mother her own mother.

It seemed that by moving back home and giving up music the client was trying to take care of her mother, identifying with her grandmother, who had suffered such an early loss. After this unconscious loyalty and bonding love was acknowledged in the constellation, there was a shift for everybody. The grandmother felt seen, the mother also relaxed and the client felt freer to pursue her own life.

In a second step the client was then invited to ask her mother to allow her to love her father too and play music. Then she thanked her father and told him that she would now play her own kind of music.

Finally, she could also honour her former band and what she had received from playing with them, but at the same time told them that she would now start playing her own kind of songs.

Creativity is really a discontinuity with the past. Parents always represent the past and one needs to learn to leave them behind and move towards the future alone. To loosen family bonds is not easy, but unless we are ready to be alone, without wanting the support from our parents, we cannot really give birth to ourselves, which is the highest creative act. It also means giving up personal desires and wishes and being more in tune with what life has to offer. Meditation is a way to find such a deep 'yes' inside.

Session 2

A female artist reports that whenever she is creative there comes a moment afterwards where she feels destructive. During the session, it showed that her creativity was out of effort, not out of joy. She had a goal in mind that she wanted to achieve. Often such goals are connected to a childhood trauma, where we did not get enough recognition from our parents as a child and this need for recognition keeps running our life. And the tragedy is that no recognition that we may get now can fill the hole, because it is not related to the present, but to a childhood wound.

She was not focused on her own joy, but on getting appreciation. And, of course, simultaneously her frustration and anger grew, which she repressed, and once in a while it burst out. In the work, we first helped her not to fight her anger, but understand it as a consequence of not respecting herself. When she could consciously allow her anger, she felt more vital and also realised that she had been afraid of what she had called 'destructive'. Now she could start to enjoy her own energy more and give up any future goal. In that moment, the effort to achieve recognition and the anger both disappeared simultaneously.

True creativity is not an achievement or an effort to get anything and it is not related to a personal desire. It depends more on our ability to let go and allow the energy of life to flow through us unhindered. So, the real question is whether we are doing an activity for its own sake or expecting to get a particular outcome. Are we enjoying the work we do, or are we more interested in the money or recognition we get from it?
"Creativity is out of nothingness. The more you are a nobody, the more you know that there is no ego in you, the more creativity will flow through you." (Osho)

An incident from a training with Meera

Samarpan, a participant in one of Meera's painting trainings relates this story: It used to happen that many artists attended Meera's painting training. Once during a painting session, one of these artists had painted a beautiful lotus flower that appeared to be just perfect. She happily sat before her picture and waited for further instructions from Meera. When Meera passed by and asked her to continue her painting, the artist replied that she did not know what else to do as her painting was finished. Meera asked her to close her eyes, took a big brush with black paint and made a big black splash on the picture. Then she asked the participant to open her eyes. The artist had tears in her eyes, her painting was destroyed! Meera said: "This is how life is! It is never finished. It is wild and unexpected. Now go with it and continue!"

Samarpan remembers being shocked about Meera's wildness and her way of transmitting a message. She didn't know what to say about the wild content of the message! She now realised how her own painting was a mirror of her whole life, how carefully she tried to control the colours and shapes and avoided those parts that did not look beautiful in her eyes. Suddenly, she dared to take a risk, used a big brush and enjoyed following her energy without being too concerned about the outcome. Later, when Meera passed by, she showed her how nothing that she had painted earlier was ever lost and how to look at any outcome with fresh eyes and discover the beauty in the spontaneous, unplanned happenings on the paper. She learned that a painting can always be continued, that it is like life, an ongoing stream of events and what we judge as ugly may turn out mysteriously beautiful and that we are always free to change any time we want.

Review

For some people, trauma induces creativity, while another's ability to be creative can be shattered by a traumatic event. Certainly, when one is creative, this brings about post-traumatic growth, but we also need to consider how to define creativity, whether the creative expression is more of a mental catharsis or an authentic creative expression that arises from a meditative consciousness. Creativity does not only relate to artistic activities, as it is not related to any act in particular, but to the quality we bring to the act. Any mundane activity can be done creatively, just as any artistic activity can also be done in an uncreative way. If we do anything creatively, we will always feel a freshness, a spontaneity and aliveness that comes with it. The more alive a person is, the more creative he will be and he will always invent new ways of doing things. And learning to be creative brings us in deep communion with life and can restore our inner health.

Part III: Working with People

After having discussed some key elements in understanding trauma and how to support someone in healing a traumatic experience, I want to end this book by briefly discussing some of the qualities a helper needs in order to do this and how his own unprocessed trauma can get in the way. Many helpers suffer from what is called 'compassion fatigue.' They themselves may become traumatised when listening to their client's trauma (secondary traumatisation) or their own unresolved traumatic past might be triggered. Therefore, besides knowing a therapeutic method, one needs to have a level of self-awareness and inner clarity about one's own unresolved traumas, as well as one's personal strength and weakness.

Chapter Twelve

Principles of Working with People

In my first two books, *The Zen Way of Counseling* and *The Roots of Love*, I have discussed the therapeutic attitude and the therapist-client relationship and have outlined principles of how to support a client's healing journey. Here, I will only summarise a few points and emphasise what I consider especially important when dealing with trauma issues.

Compassion and presence are the two main ingredients in any therapeutic work, more important than technical skills. It is, however, essential to comprehend the meaning of compassion, which can often remain vague and is just left to common assumptions. Words like 'love' or 'compassion' often camouflage hidden motives, and then talking about being 'compassionate' can become part of a conditioned response that can be quite contrary to its authentic meaning.

Compassion

In our upbringing, we are usually taught that we should be kind, sensitive and considerate of others. Compassion becomes part of our cultivated behaviour rather than being a spontaneous outpouring of our heart. Such compassion cannot be authentic and cannot touch another person on a deeper level. True compassion and love cannot be taught as they are part of our original nature and therefore arise spontaneously when we start living a more conscious, meditative life.

If a therapist or helper treats a client with kindness, as is expected of him, this certainly can help the client to feel more at ease and relaxed, but it may just stay on the level of social conformity and then it will not reach the other on a deeper level, where he feels truly met and understood. Compassion should arise from a true center and not be just a cultivated and learned response.

I remember how, in the weeks after Meera's passing, some people offered their condolences to me and how uncomfortable and sometimes disturbing this actually felt. I sometimes had the impression that those people just did not know what to do or say and filled that moment of not knowing with platitudes that did not arise inside them as an authentic response. On the other hand, there were people who could just remain silent or look at me or hug me or they cried with me and that said much more than any words could have expressed.

Love or compassion naturally arise in us when we become more centered in our heart. If we act from an idea or concept of what we should do, even when it comes with the intention of helping someone, it is still bound to be false and inauthentic. A therapist may become bored listening to his client's life story and rather than respecting this feeling and bringing his client to the present moment, he may force himself to be attentive and 'empathetic'. This does not lead to inner transformation, but may only deepen a client's identification with his mind. Superficially, he may enjoy the attention, but such listening will give more energy to the mind and further deepen the split from his heart or being.

A spiritual therapist will strengthen his client's connection with his body, heart and being rather than remaining in the dimension of the mind. In order to be able to do this, he himself needs to be connected to his own heart and inner being. Technical skill is one thing, but to be an authentic individual is another. Being a therapist is just a role one adopts for a certain time and behind that role is one's true reality, that always shines through at each moment. There are people in whose presence one feels uplifted and almost healed, even if they may not be trained in a therapeutic method and there are others in whose presence one may feel energetically drained, even though they are technically skilful. This can happen whether anything is said or not.

Authentic compassion is more connected to honesty than to being nice, superficially friendly or pleasing. Even when confronting someone with a seemingly harsh truth, this may prove to be more compassionate than acting in a socially 'correct' way or following a textbook intervention. In trauma therapy we learn how to resource a client and calm his overcharged nervous system, which is certainly helpful, but this should not just remain a professional attitude, but become part of a therapist's authentic response. The mystic Osho in one of his discourses stated that a therapist has to learn much in order to be of help and then he has to be able to forget all he knows (in order to help). He has to do something seemingly very contradictory.

Being true to oneself may not always be in tune with a professional code of conduct. In my own experience as a participant in many trainings, I never felt truly 'resourced' or met by therapists who may have been skilful in their method, but lacked deeper presence as an individual.

Presence

It is now obvious that compassion and presence are closely related. Presence is the quality of being available in the present moment, alert to whatever is happening, without being distracted by accumulated knowledge, theory, or by thinking about the past or future. Many mystics have described this quality of 'being present' as a state of meditation.

Presence for a therapist can mean two things:

1. Being ready to give up any pre-conceived ideas developed during the course of one's work with previous clients and their problems, and being able to look at each new person with fresh eyes, addressing the situation as if one has never seen a case like this before.

2. To be ready to give up any plan, any pre-formulated idea, any notion about what may be 'good' for the client. What is good for a client is not something the therapist can know; in fact, like the rest of us, he cannot really know what is good for anybody, other than perhaps himself. One may have ideas about it, and all therapists usually do, but ultimately there is no way to know ahead of time what will work, or not work, for other people.

If a therapist is able to do these two things – forget about the past and future, and relax into not-knowing – a quality of presence arises naturally. In this state, the therapist does not need anything from the client and, once he has no expectations, he can relax and accept the situation simply as it is.

Compassion and love are then experienced in a new way because presence and lovingness go hand in hand, they occur at the same time and they are either both absent or both present. Compassion arises naturally out of presence, and real presence is not a cold or detached state, but is full of warmth and care. You are conscious of yourself and the client at the same time. It could be best described as 'cool love', in the sense that one can remain calm, even when a client reports difficult or painful experiences.

There are practical ways that can help a person to attain or maintain presence. One is to be conscious of your own body and physical sensations, including your body posture and rhythm of breathing. The body is always in the Here and Now, so if we are aware of our body we have to be in the moment. The mind is always thinking of the past or future and how to attain a desired goal. In that sense, if a therapist is overly concerned with how to help a client to feel better and improve his condition, he loses presence. In a strange way, this means that the more we try to help someone, the more we lose presence and the more real help becomes difficult or impossible. Real help is always very indirect and cannot be approached directly. The more a therapist gives up his intention to help or to achieve a certain outcome in the session, the more his client is helped in a deeper sense.

This dynamic is often not understood by people working in the helping professions, which may be the reason why sometimes clients are not really helped, in spite of every good intention. Moreover, when one tries to offer help in the ordinary sense, the helper will eventually feel exhausted and drained. We will come back to this point in the next chapter.

Besides connecting to our body in order to find presence, it can also be helpful to be in touch with our heart, not the physical heart, but the energetic heart center in the middle of the chest. By being connected to the heart center, one also finds a state of inner balance and a deep acceptance of everything as it is. This is not an emotional state, but a state of peacefulness, where desires become less important. This state is therefore also called the 'empty heart', in order to distinguish it from the emotional state of love.

Sometimes, the mind can also be used to find presence, for example when we consciously try to remember a moment or past situation when we were centered or experienced a moment of being without thought. This could have been a moment of meditation or a situation where an outer event caught us by surprise to the extent that, for an instant, our mind stopped functioning. When we consciously remember such a moment, we can sometimes reconnect with that experience of being without thought and some flavour of it can come back to us in the present. It is indeed possible to actively invite a state of presence. It may not necessarily be a very deep, meditative or transcendental state, but it may be enough to help us and a client to be less identified with a problem and the constant stream of thoughts.

'Centering' is a form of self-observation, where we watch our own internal process moment-to-moment. It is a vital ingredient in any therapy practice because it enables a therapist to approach the client and his life without prejudice, expectations, or preconceived ideas. It is a state of relaxed alertness that prevents a therapist from being caught up in 'helping' or 'saving' someone or assuming a personal point of view. It means remaining aware of one's own state of consciousness and therefore not getting lost in the client and the client's issues, or being concerned about reaching a particular outcome in the session.

Non-Identification

Therapists in general tend to identify with their own area of expertise and their preferred therapeutic method. A Freudian analyst tends to see repressed sexuality at the roots of all problems, an Adlerian analyst sees an Adlerian analyst sees will to power. A systemic therapist may see trans-generational entanglements behind his client's problems and a trauma therapist may discover unresolved traumas at the root of his client's issues. Being overly identified with a certain psychological method or approach is like wearing coloured glasses, and then the whole world appears accordingly.

Not all psychological issues are related to a past trauma and even if there was a trauma in a client's past, it may already have been healed and integrated. When a trauma trained therapist is very identified with his method of expertise, he may treat everyone as if he is traumatised, needs support and should be protected from confrontation or any form of intensity. It is not rare to see trauma therapists cautioning their clients against active or cathartic meditations and treating their client as if they were walking on eggshells. This may certainly be appropriate at times and clearly the impact of trauma has been gravely neglected in therapy in the past. It is, however, important for a therapist to notice whether his intervention arises from the fear of retraumatising his client. Fear or too much concern are not a good base for any intervention and they are likely to increase the fear in the client rather than help him to overcome it.

A systemic therapist on the other hand may tend to prematurely examine his client's family history without considering whether his client is in a stable enough condition to allow him to deal with a traumatic family past. Overlooking the tremendous impact of trauma on body and mind may lead a systemic therapist to confront a client too soon or too suddenly with a family trauma, rather than accompanying him more slowly through states of activation or dissociation. This can then indeed become retraumatising for the client.

It is a delicate art to find the appropriate balance between giving support and confronting a client with a painful past. A therapist needs to create a safe space for his client without taking over any responsibility for his life and for what he needs to face and deal with. A painful or traumatic event should neither be addressed too soon nor should facing it be postponed too long.

Being less identified with one's personal training and technique and having processed one's own past wounds will help a therapist to respond to his client's needs with flexibility and avoid falling into the trap of seeing his client's issue through the coloured glasses that any system or theory inevitably provides. We will come back to this topic in the following chapter.

No Intention

Not only do therapists identify with their area of expertise, but clients also are identified with their own problems and issues. They are often convinced that this is who they are, or they identify with a person from their family system, as constellation work reveals.

Identification in general is at the root of all problems. We identify with our bodies and our minds and are often unable to remain a witness to the events that happen to these bodies and minds. The stronger or deeper such identifications are, the less capacity we have to just observe what is happening, the more difficult or even impossible it can be to process and finally resolve an issue.

The desire for change is directly related to the degree of identification we feel.

While clients naturally have a desire for change, the therapist should have no such intention, or at least be unconcerned if a desired outcome is reached or not. This may sound strange to some therapists and psychologists, who work for the welfare of their clients, and scientific studies are usually conducted to evaluate the effectiveness of a therapeutic intervention. On a superficial level, this kind of help is meaningful, but on a deeper existential level real help only becomes possible if the desire for help has been abandoned. Only then does a therapist's intervention come from presence and carry the quality of acceptance that is free of any hidden motives. By being in a deep inner agreement with his client's life situation as it is, a therapist will be more able to respond spontaneously to his client moment to moment. Essentially a therapist is mirroring what is going on inside his client and this function can be more clearly carried out if he has no intention. True inner transformation only happens when we are in a state of deep acceptance; it is spontaneous and not the result of forced effort.

No Fear

Often transformation and shifts in consciousness happen when we reach a certain cul-de-sac in our life, a point where we cannot go any further, like a pendulum that changes direction when it has reached its furthest point, its peak. For example, sometimes we only realise that success cannot give us happiness after we have reached a higher rank on the ladder of success. Before that, we may still have great hopes and dreams that push us to keep going. At the peak point of success there is nowhere else to go.

In therapy, we often accompany a client to such an extreme and introduce an awareness of all the consequences of his actions instead of asking him to change or trying to prematurely save him from what appears to be a bad outcome. It is better to show an ambitious person how his body is suffering and getting sick, rather than trying to convince him to drop his ambitions. Being confronted with a painful reality may lead to the realisation that one has been living in a dream and only when one can abandon all hope can authentically change and inner transformation take place.

For the therapist, it is therefore necessary to embrace an attitude of being unafraid of what may happen to his client and be in a deep inner agreement with his life's path, even if this may lead him towards suffering, and even death. It sounds paradoxical, but only if I agree that someone wants to take his own life, can I help to save his life.

In therapy, there are two kinds of approaches: In one, the therapist gives hope to the client, helps him not to give up and supports his trust that change is possible.

In the other, he takes all hope away from the client, because only at the point where he no longer has any hope and is facing reality as it is, can transformation take place.

It all depends on what is necessary for a client at a particular moment. Traumatised people often find themselves in a state of hopelessness, which is not a state of acceptance, but of giving up, because they have been overwhelmed by a traumatic event and the course of their lives, including all their desires have been thwarted. They did not let go of desires and hopes out of understanding, but because an existential event took away all possibility of achieving a desired goal. So giving up is really a negative state, where hopes and desires are only repressed or hidden. In therapy, this first needs to be brought back into the light of awareness and only then can a true let-go become a possibility.

If a therapist is able to agree and be unafraid of whatever may happen to his client, he can help him to face reality as it is rather than trying to save him from it. For example, it is usually better to confront a person with a terminal illness with the fact that he is not likely to survive very long rather than giving him the hope that he will be healed. The power of the healing sentences used in constellation work, for example, result from the fact that they are short, direct and point to a bare fact without any sugar-coating. When therapists act from fear or avoid confronting their clients with reality, they cannot be of much help.

Non-seriousness

Maintaining an inner attitude of playfulness and non-seriousness is maybe one of the most important, but also one of the rarest qualities to be found amongst helpers and therapists. When we are non-serious and can still smile or laugh at ourselves, then we are really in a meditative, non-attached state of consciousness. This lightness of being is maybe one of the qualities that is most missed in our everyday life and even spiritual seekers and so-called meditators tend to take themselves and whatever happens with a serious attitude that often shows a deep level of identification. Responding to a client with sincerity, but without becoming serious, is really a beautiful art.

Chapter Thirteen

The Trauma of the Helper

People in the helping professions are also affected by their own personal traumas and it can easily happen that when a therapist is confronted with his client's trauma, his own unresolved traumatic past gets triggered. For example, when a therapist, who was sexually abused in childhood, listens to his client's history of abuse, his own unprocessed feelings of rage, panic or pain may surface. It is not rare to see therapists identifying with victims of abuse and wishing punishment for the perpetrator. The moment a helper identifies with a victim's hidden anger or shame, or a perpetrator's hidden guilt, he is unable to help a client to find a resolution that serves their healing.

Contacting anger is valuable only because it takes a person out of a dissociated state and out of feeling helpless, but it is not the real healing. Healing happens when one is able to grow beyond anger and find a deep 'yes' to life and that is true for both clients and therapists. Helpers sometimes have a tendency to take the role of a protector and want to give a client what they themselves have missed. This urge to help others is sometimes referred to as the 'helper syndrome' and has its roots in an early childhood wound. We will discuss this further below.

When the client's trauma triggers the therapist's own trauma, he will be facing his own unprocessed charge and will then have to deal with his own arousal and find ways to regulate himself before he can be of any support to his client. It may not be immediately clear whether the activation that a therapist feels when dealing with a client's trauma is arising because of his own undigested history or whether it is a consequence of resonating with his client in the present.

What is Resonance?

Resonance is an important therapeutic tool that gives therapists an insight into what is happening with a client. It can be best described as the ability of human beings to sense each other, regulate each other and communicate with each by means other than the five senses, but also including the five senses. Such a synchronisation between therapist or helper and his client can happen on a physical, emotional, energetic and cognitive level. In other words, one can sense the physical sensations of another person in one's own body, including physical signs of activation. One can feel the feelings of another person in oneself and one can have similar thoughts or memories to the other. It basically means that it is possible to pick up the energy of another person and experience what is happening to the other as if it were happening to oneself.

We humans share this capacity with other mammals who create social systems, and that gives us a certain survival advantage in the sense that we can feel things already before they actually happen to us, just because they happened to another member of our group. If a member of our group is in danger, we can already feel the danger at an early stage before it even reaches us, just because we are in resonance. Because of resonance, a mother knows what is happening to her child without anyone needing to tell her about it.

This ability to be in resonance can serve as a therapeutic tool, as a therapist can feel what is going on in his client even before the client is conscious of it himself. It can also become a blueprint for the potential development of the client, as through resonance the therapist can process an energy that was overwhelming for the client and mirror this back to him. It is similar to how a mother can help her child to process a painful experience by absorbing it within herself, while retaining her calm presence and thus being a resource for the child. In a similar way, the calm and soothing presence of a therapist, who is able to process in himself the activation he may pick up from his client, can serve as a learning on how to process a charge in the client's own nervous system.

So, resonance is a diagnostic tool and a healing remedy as well. However, as resonance happens both ways, from the client to the therapist and from the therapist to the client, it can potentially happen that the activation of the client may overwhelm the therapist and rather than being a healing force, he may get more charged, which then will further activate the client. In other words, two unregulated systems move more and more into dysregulation. One can observe this when watching the interaction of two hurt or angry people and how they sometimes gradually move more and more into feeling wounded and angry.

Especially in the case of learning to handle trauma, a helper or therapist needs to be well regulated and able to process any activation that happens to him while listening to his client in order to avoid being pulled into the trauma energy. In order to accomplish this, one needs to be aware of subtle changes in one's own body chemistry, because it is in the body where the first signs of activation happen. It is easy to get lost in the client's story, especially when he reports dramatic events, and forget to remain rooted in the Here and Now. More important than the story itself is how one is related to those past events, how one feels about it now and how the body reacts in the present moment while the story is being told.

Compassion fatigue

It can be physically and emotionally exhausting just to listen to the trauma stories of clients. To help them process their physiological activation further can be challenging. Providing care or therapeutic help to people who have suffered traumatic events can lead to a secondary stress reaction, or secondary traumatic stress in the caregiver. This is sometimes called compassion fatigue or vicarious trauma and refers to the negative emotions that may emerge as a consequence of helping victims of trauma. It is different from burnout, which can occur in any profession and develops over time as an accumulated stress. Compassion fatigue on the other hand can happen more suddenly and is usually more likely to affect health professionals.

The empathy a helper feels for his client can also make him susceptible to identifying with what happened and as a consequence the helper's own body-mind system can become exhausted or he may develop symptoms of post-traumatic stress, even though the trauma did not happen to him personally. When one is dealing with several clients in a day and being confronted with their emotional stress, this can easily overwhelm a helper's capacity.

Good intentions are certainly not enough and one must develop meditative presence, clear emotional boundaries and be able to care for oneself. This, together with living a balanced lifestyle, are some of the measures that can prevent compassion fatigue. As we discussed earlier, authentic compassion does not arise from sacrificing oneself for others, but is rooted in compassion for oneself.

Establishing clear boundaries

It is especially important for anyone who works with traumatised clients to maintain clear personal boundaries and to be sensitive to the boundaries of clients. As described in Chapter Six, traumatised people often suffered boundary violations, in particular if they are dealing with bonding traumas. As a consequence, they either lack the sense of their own boundaries or they are unable to assert them and maintain their ground. This can relate to physical, emotional, intellectual or sexual boundaries. At the same time, they may not be so conscious of the boundaries of the therapist or helper and may show a tendency to intrude into the therapist's space and privacy.[4] It is important to remember that neither the desire of a client to create a personal relationship with his therapist, nor such a desire from the side of the therapist, is appropriate. However, a therapist should have the capacity to deal with it when such desires emerge or take personal supervision if he notices his own limitation to do so.

---

[4] The famous movie *What about Bob?* is a perfect example for boundary violations between therapist and client and to what consequences this may lead.

Rather than identifying with a client, a helper needs to be very clear about his own boundaries and, with sensitivity, assert them. This includes not being available 24 hours a day for a client, respecting the therapeutic contract and timing of a session, as well as not exaggeratedly talking about events from one's own private life. It should be clear that the therapist-client relationship is not like a personal friendship and the boundaries between one's private and professional life need to be distinct.

While the clarity of the therapist may help a client to become more conscious of boundaries on different levels, the therapist may also address this issue with his client more directly and help the client to become more sensitive to what makes him feel comfortable or when he starts feeling disturbed. Small exercises to practice saying 'no', 'stop' or allowing oneself to retreat or move forward, as well as establishing the 'fight' response on a physiological level can be part of this learning process.

Physical touch is a delicate issue with trauma clients and while it can promote a faster healing and discharge, it can also lead to activation and bring up memories of old boundary violations. Therefore, physical touch should be used with special awareness; the purpose of it should be explained and the client should be asked if and how they like to be touched. Touching extremities and bony parts of the body like a shoulder or hand is usually preferable.

If a therapy process includes a series of sessions, then timing and time intervals between sessions should be made clear, as well as when and how a client can contact his therapist.

The 'helper syndrome'

Anyone in the helping professions should have a certain awareness of why he has chosen this profession in the first place. Hidden or unconscious motives often lead to interventions that do not serve the client, but fulfil a helper's own needs. One should be especially aware of a basic human need, the need to be loved and appreciated. When this is very pronounced, as it often is in helpers, it can lead to a strong desire to rescue others from pain or suffering.

The psychology behind this 'helper syndrome' is a deep need to be needed and an unconscious wish to rescue one's own parent, in particular one's mother, from pain and suffering. Commonly, people with such tendencies had a mother who was unable to properly attend to their needs in childhood, maybe because she herself could not recover from a personal trauma. As a consequence, they developed a care taking attitude towards their own mother, sacrificing their own needs in an unconscious effort to get their mother's attention and appreciation. They learned to make themselves indispensable to someone else in order to make sure the other continued to need them. This strategy can be best described as 'giving to get'.

When such children grow up, they develop a certain style of relating with others, where they tend to be in a care taking role and that is also why they often choose a career as a health professional. Because they developed a special sensitivity towards the needs of others early in life, they often have special caretaking skills that they unconsciously use to get their own needs fulfilled in an indirect way. They care for a client because they really would like to be taken care of. This focus on the other leads to a neglect of their own needs and of taking responsibility for fulfilling them. Therefore, while trying to save or rescue others, they often forget their own needs or ignore their own capacities and boundaries. By feeling needed, they unconsciously try to fulfil their desire to receive love and appreciation. Initially, neither client nor helper may notice this, but after a while clients may react to the helper's unconscious expectations and become angry or upset, often to the surprise of the helper, who does not understand why the client got upset as he was caring so 'selflessly'.

Sometimes, people in the helping professions suffer from this pattern, in which they give up themselves for their clients or try to give to others what they themselves would need. They may even risk their own health or joy for the welfare of others. Chronic helpers are often not very happy people in their private lives and we find the highest suicide rate of all the professions in the helping professions. The underlying psychology is that by leaving one's own welfare behind and caring for others, one will at least feel loved, appreciated and be considered valuable and worthy. Not many other careers offer such a great possibility of receiving this level of gratification as the helping professions.

Healing the 'helper syndrome' and the unworthiness wound

In life it is quite common that we give, not because we are in a state of overflow, but because we want to get something from the other. To feel a personal need is uncomfortable and we tend to avoid showing it to others, but prefer to be in the role of the giver, which is more gratifying and ego fulfilling. For a child it sometimes is the only strategy available that helps him get some attention from his primary caretaker and be considered a 'good' child. By not showing his need and instead supporting his parent, he manages to survive and receive some of the love and appreciation he really longs for. This works for a child as a survival strategy, but also fixates him in a painful situation, where he also needs to repress what he really needs and wants. So, a part of him always remains empty and unfulfilled.

The real change for someone with such a pattern comes when he starts to expose his real needs, which can almost feel like dying to him. Acknowledging this wound and exposing it, is often the first step towards healing. After all, it is not his fault that he had parents who were traumatised themselves and could not attend to his needs in childhood. But rather than seeing any fault in their parents, children have a tendency to blame themselves for what their parents could not do. This can lead to a deep feeling of unworthiness, a feeling as if something is basically wrong with me. Such existential shame can become deeply rooted in our psychology and is at the core of many psychological issues that we carry since childhood. For a child to be needy is his existential condition.

Accepting and respecting this is an important step towards further growth. However, even for many adults, to be called 'needy' can cause deep shame and can lead to a feeling of wanting to hide or disappear. This part inside us, where we feel needy, wounded and unfulfilled remains there until we learn to open up to it.

But we often prefer to avoid this and for some people even the wish to have a child can be one of the ways to cover a deep-rooted feeling of unworthiness. If someone like that gives birth to a child, then this child is not born because his parents had an overflowing energy that they wanted to share, but because they felt an inner emptiness that they wanted to fill with the presence of a child, who would love them unconditionally. People sometimes even advise others to have a child if they feel unfulfilled or have a sense of meaninglessness in their lives. From the very beginning, such a child will be burdened with the unconscious expectations from his parents that he is meant to fulfil.

In a constellation, this becomes visible when, for example, the representative of a parent is overly focused on his child or even moves towards the child. This can be an indication that the parent has expectations of his child and can't really see the child for who he is. Then the child's existential state of being receptive to his parents and for parents to give to their child is reversed and suffering arises. Such unhealthy interactions between parents and children can often be traced back many generations, where in each generation a child could not get something from his parent and as a result tries to get from his own child, who then again will do the same to his children.

This is how suffering gets passed on from one generation to the next – or one could say, how earlier traumas travel from one generation to the next. Children are always born with an unconditional love for their parents, a bonding love, which ensures their survival. This desire to bond with their parents makes them ready to suffer, risk their health or even die for their parents.

The second step in healing, after learning to sense and expose one's true need, requires a readiness to face the unpleasant feelings of frustration, anger or sometimes despair and loneliness that come up if such needs are not responded to. In other words, one needs to learn to process such unpleasant feelings in a safe setting, like a therapy session for example.

A client may not be grateful for the overly caring attitude of his therapist. A friend or partner may not respond in a loving or caring way to one's expectations. Or success and respectability may turn into its opposite. Any situation like this can potentially bring up anger, frustration and a feeling of emptiness that one had managed to keep hidden sometimes since childhood. It takes courage to face and pass through such dark moments alone, which is also part of the healing process. Only when one is willing to do this, can one reach a deeper self-connection, free from all superficial niceness or pleasing attitudes, towards clients as well. Now a more authentic compassion can appear that is born out of feeling respect and compassion for oneself. Only a person who has gone through such a process can be an authentic therapist or helper. Because now he no longer needs to receive the acknowledgment and appreciation of his clients, at least not on an existential level to prop up his self-esteem. Now he will not make sacrifices and lose contact with his own truth. Being in contact with one's own joy and inner fulfilment makes a therapist capable of truly sharing such experiences with a client.

Everyone has a unique quality that he can bring to the work and share with others. By dealing with a traumatic past successfully, one also develops a special skill and ability that can contribute to one's work with people. When we learned as a child to be sensitive to the needs of our parents, then this sensitivity can become a special skill that allows us to know the needs of a client, sometimes even before he is aware of it himself. When such sensitivity is combined with the ability to take care of one's own needs rather than wanting them to be fulfilled from outside, then this can be the formula for being a good therapist. I define a good therapist as someone who knows how to enjoy himself in each moment, who is in touch with what fulfils him and yet is sensitive towards the other.

Only a truly fulfilled person has something authentic to share and can be of benefit to someone else. Centering, understood in this way, makes one capable of accompanying another through his own inner turmoil without being taken over by his pain, fear or anger. In the previous chapter, I defined this as a state of presence that is different from an ordinary helper mentality. What is helpful in a therapeutic sense is distinct from what is ordinarily understood as help. It is not a rescue, but an escorting. Any suffering a client undergoes may bring about a level of consciousness that he may not reach if someone else tries to save him from it.

Examples from sessions

A female therapist came for a session because she felt exhausted in her work with people. She suffered from a feeling of never being good enough, which was also the reason why she kept on studying continuously, but still always felt something was lacking. The session revealed a strong desire to get approval from her parents, especially her father, while at the same time wanting to help him with a past trauma. Since childhood she had tried to be a 'good girl' and not give her parents, who also were also in economic difficulties, any trouble. The desire to help them contributed to her choosing to become a therapist.

In the session, we worked on learning to get less involved in her parents' life experiences, honouring what they had to pass through, while at the same time becoming more conscious of what she really enjoyed doing in her own life. When she looked at her parents and ancestors, who had passed through various traumas, and could understand that they felt relieved to see her live a happy life, she also felt relief and could now receive their blessings for pursuing her own life. Now helping others was no longer out of sacrificing herself or to get approval, but became more a sharing of the love that she could feel for her family and herself.

In another session, a male client's issue was that he suffered from anxiety. A constellation revealed the hidden aggression that he had taken over from his father and grandfather, who were in the Spanish civil war and had to fight against family members on the opposite side. Anxiety and aggression were part of the unresolved trauma response, the fight and flight responses that continued to be active in him, something he could not understand when only looking at his personal life history. Respecting both parties in the civil war and their suffering, while at the same time acknowledging that all belonged to the same country and nation, brought him relief and also served the reconciliation that still needed to happen between the two factions. So this session was only partly to relieve him from anxiety, but partly also to help him learn to carry feelings that come as a consequence of belonging to a certain family system.

Helping the Helper

In my trainings, participants who prepare themselves for working with people learn about the difference between these two kinds of helping and develop the understanding that true empathy starts with empathy for oneself. Therefore, learning what presence is, what meditation means and how to overcome personal traumas and find personal fulfilment and joy in life are essential preparation for learning to work with people.

A child, who is trying to help his parents, is called a parental child, as he tries to be a parent to his own parent. Similarly, therapists sometimes take a parental role towards their clients, who on the other hand like to project an ideal parent onto the therapist. This is called transference and countertransference in psychological terms and doesn't lead to personal maturity. Instead it strengthens unhealthy bonding. In the work of Family Constellation, we try to discourage such behaviour and help people to loosen their bonding to their family members, by first respecting the existence of such bonds and then finding ways to grow beyond them. This often needs time and goes hand in hand with healing traumatic wounds of the past. Only when we feel a certain freedom in relation to our parents and family members will we not unconsciously create similar bonds to our clients or allow them to bond with us in similar ways. Then we feel less responsibility towards clients and more respect at the same time. In turn, clients will feel more respected and more self-responsible.

As clients sometimes inevitably trigger the trauma of the therapist, a therapist needs to learn to be well connected to his own body and its self-regulating mechanism. This will also help him to avoid misinterpreting being centered with being cut off. It is not rare to find therapists in a dissociated state without noticing it, but instead believing themselves to be present and unaffected. A therapist, who mainly works from knowledge or intellectual understanding is really in a dissociated state, because he is disconnected from his heart and feelings. Empathy is not an intellectual state and as such cannot be studied, only developed over time. That is why simply studying a subject, whether it is about trauma or anything else is not enough. One cannot learn to work with people in the same way as one learns to drive a car. Studying at university and also just reading this book is not enough in itself to prepare one to work with trauma.

I always include cathartic meditations in my trainings and courses because they work on the physical and emotional level both. Meditation should include all levels of being, body, mind, heart and then move beyond. Only doing silent or sitting meditations, even though helpful in many ways, can sometimes make a person become more dissociated and can make him bypass his own emotional issues.

Finally, I want to mention the importance for a good therapist or helper of also being connected to a transcendental or impersonal state of being, because only then will his interventions not come from his own personality, which is always limiting. Moreover, he will not be so self-conscious about his work and neither feel too great if his session turns out well, nor too terrible if it doesn't. Our personality is shaped by our conditioning and traumatic past and this in one way or another creates limitations. For example, a therapist who has been shamed in the past tends to either become shaming or pleasing with his clients.

In a deeper sense, a session is not about being in contact with someone else, but about coming more in contact with oneself, with all the layers of one's personality and beyond. Therefore, a truly therapeutic relationship is more of a 'no-relationship'. Only when therapists do not have a need for contact, can they give freedom to their client, the freedom to be in contact or not, to be in the mind and dissociated or to be available to the Here and Now. Any goal from the side of the therapist about where a session should go becomes a subtle infringement on the client's freedom and space. Therefore, one ultimately needs to let go of any idea that there needs to be some kind of completion, or 'happy ending', or for some kind of resolution.

Whether healing will happen or not always remains unknown and in the hands of an existential force. A therapist needs to be in agreement with this, even if it is contrary to his training, psychological concepts or theories. Then each session can be a learning as much for the helper or therapist as for his client.

Epilogue

A Personal Note about Living and Dying

In Chapter Two, I have mentioned that most people don't really face the fact that their life in this physical body is limited and use dissociation as a strategy for dealing with the subject of death. Death is perceived in the context of old age, sickness and suffering and therefore it creates the feeling that it is something to be avoided, or at least pushed as far away as possible. Health advertisements promise long life if you buy their products, assuming that this is people's ultimate goal, while dying early is really a misfortune that happens to the unlucky ones. It appears that in our society long life matters more than quality of life.

We see in constellation sessions how the early death of family members creates not only suffering and pain in the ones, who remain behind, but also a deep-rooted sense that something has gone wrong. Most of us are not, or only vaguely, aware of the truth that life as such is so vast and gives such a variety of destinies to people, including a short life span for some and a long one for others and this contains no evaluation as such. However, it is really our deep-rooted bonding that does not allow us to cope effectively with a painful event. For example, if a mother is overly influenced by the idea that her child belongs to her, almost as an extension of herself, then if this child should suddenly die, it will be very difficult, or almost impossible for her to cope with the loss.

It certainly took me a very long time to let go of the torturous thoughts of what had gone wrong in Meera's accident, what I 'should' have done differently and of all the things that 'should' not have gone the way they did from the start. From an ordinary perspective, my and others' mistakes are obvious, but to grasp the wider context, where also this was meant to happen, not just as a spiritual idea, but a deep realisation, is not so easy and will still take time for me. To move from 'should' to the isness of life needs a letting go of personal desires and preferences.

Developing a meditative awareness seems essential in learning to cope with the loss of a loved one. It includes a remembrance that we are all part of a cosmic drama, in which each one of us has a certain role to play that we are often not free to choose. There is a small meditation that can be of help to be less identified with a role or activity we are engaged in.

Meditation (from Vigyan Bhairav Tantra Vol I, 6.th technique)

WHEN IN WORLDLY ACTIVITY, KEEP ATTENTIVE BETWEEN THE TWO BREATHS, AND SO PRACTICING, IN A FEW DAYS, BE BORN ANEW.
  This simple technique can be done at any time while doing any small ordinary activity, like walking or eating or anything else. Keep on doing the activity and keep one part of your attention on the small gap that exists between each in- and out-breath.
  Osho comments that this meditation can help break the identification with an activity or any given role and practicing this meditation over a long time, one eventually learns to see one's whole life as an endless drama, as if one is just an actor playing a certain role.

And ultimately one will be able to experience all life events as if they are happening to someone else.

Over time, with meditation, one learns to be less identified with the dramas of life and understand how everything and everyone is just playing a part in it. One slowly develops a certain subtle acceptance, an inner 'yes' and sense of gratitude that remains present somewhere deep inside even in the worst traumatic situation and even when at first it seems inaccessible. This is not a defeatist attitude, neither the acceptance of someone who has given up, as happens to people who have been overwhelmed by trauma, nor just a spiritual concept, but a truly positive attitude towards what life brings.

To lose a loved one is certainly a very painful event for anyone, but if we genuinely love the person, then we are also able to consider what will be helpful and healing for the one who has died or is about to die. People who only consider their own loss and that their wish to stay together has been shattered, remain stuck in a self-centered attitude. Authentic love is an experience that takes one beyond the self.

The more we grow in meditativeness and love, the more we become capable of letting go of each other – and ultimately letting go of ourselves as well! Children who lose a parent early often get stuck in anger because they feel abandoned. But the deeper truth is that no one really abandons anyone because we are all bound by our own life path – whether we are a parent, a lover or a child. We are all alone here, only travelling together for the time being and, eventually, we all have to leave each other. No one can know for sure when this moment will come, but an intelligent person will try to prepare for it whenever he finds the opportunity. Reading about it or agreeing with it intellectually won't suffice.

For me, losing Meera was a huge shock, a most intense wake-up call that made me realise that a part of me had been under the illusion that life and our togetherness would continue forever. Even though our many departures and separations (because we sometimes worked in different countries) were a kind of training in how to practice let-go, I still did not live with the full awareness that anything we shared could easily be the last time of having this shared experience together. As I was painfully reminded, one cannot know what the next moment will bring.

Life truly always hangs on a thin thread that could break at any moment and it is a dangerous attitude to take anything for granted. Osho used to remind his disciples to live each moment to the fullest, only then can *let-go* become easier, only then do past and future not matter. Past and future matter for the mind because the mind's inner programme is to create safety, certainty and comfort for us. And it has done a great job during millions of years of evolution to create all kinds of technologies and all the advances in science. But it has not been able to make us more fulfilled, peaceful, joyful or loving. There has been no advancement in those areas.

As society became more settled and our lifestyle more secure, insured and guaranteed, our life has become duller and flatter. In order to experience a fulfilled life, one needs to be able to leave the mind behind, listen more to the heart and inner being and welcome all the insecurities there are in life, whether they are emotional, social, material or intellectual. It requires our readiness to live more fully and totally and go into the unknown with openness, without any guidebook on how to live rightly, or relate rightly.

The inner programme of our body and mind to keep us safe and alive at all costs is one of the most advanced achievements of nature and good as far as it goes, but it is bound to fail ultimately. Just as any engine finally is going to fail at last and end up on the scrap heap, our body and mind will also disintegrate; but before this happens, one should learn to disidentify from it, which may certainly be a life-long task. Only then can one truly learn to move beyond fear, because the fear of dying is at the root of all fears, and the basic fear of body and mind, its ultimate trauma so to speak.

Life and death are really part of one whole and neither can exist without the other. The moment one is born one starts dying as well; it is a 70 or 80-year long process. Death really accompanies us at every moment; it is always present. No past moment can ever be brought back, nor can we hold on to any beautiful experience, as it is already passing. Life's experiences have been compared to sand running through our fingers and even trying to clench our fist won't help. If we are intelligent, it would be better to keep our hands open and enjoy every single moment more fully, live more totally and be more grounded in the Here and Now. That really is the message of all the mystics.

I was very lucky to be there when Osho left his body. It was like an explosion of light and intense celebration. I was next to both my parents when they breathed their last. It was very peaceful and silent, like when someone goes into a deeper sleep. More recently, I was there when my beloved departed from this world, I was almost beside her. And even though it happened in this shocking and unprecedented way, I could still feel this huge wave of love that seemed to be spreading all around the globe, engulfing me and everyone who was connected to her. Now my hope is that one day, when my time comes, I will be able to be present there as well.

During the weeks and months after Meera's leaving, I received many messages in my silent moments that seemed to be coming directly from Meera. They always moved me to tears and connected me to a deep love and something transpersonal that I cannot explain. It seems appropriate to end this book with one of them:

"I am in a beautiful space. I can't explain it to you. My love is always with you, only my body is not. Isn't that the most important? And we practiced it many times, to be without the other and yet connected. As before, I am always with you, so you do not need to miss me. You always find me in your heart. And what I want to share with others, it will have to come through you now. And because you love me, you will know it. We are a buddy team now as you always wanted it. Now it is happening." (Meera)

And a message from the Master:

"You are being gifted, not hurt. You just don't know it yet. It is an opportunity."

Appendix

Self Help First Aid after shock trauma:

- Find a place where you feel safe and protected if possible
- Slow down, let the body be still and rest for a while, and leave anything else that you wanted to do
- Acknowledge that your body might be in shock and resist any tendency to ignore or deny the magnitude of what has happened
- Look for support if possible, like a friend or someone close by
- Focus your attention on your bodily sensations now and allow any emerging physical reactions, such as trembling or shaking
- Allow your feelings as long as they don't overwhelm you
- Do not talk about the details of what has happened to anyone, but stay more focused on the Here and Now (unless, for example, there is a medical reason for a doctor to know some details)
- Do not judge yourself and be aware that you may be in a dissociated state
- Do something that can bring your level of activation down (hot bath, touch, talking to someone as long as you feel good about it). After a while you may walk slowly and move the body

- Try as much as possible to avoid anything that can further create stress for you
- In general: Be kind to yourself and see what you need in the moment

First Aid for helping others after shock trauma:

All the above points also apply when supporting others. Further:

- Keep the body safe, lying down and warm
- Reassure the person that you will remain with him or her until they feel better
- Remind the person that he or she is safe now and the event is over and that there is nothing to do. Reassure them that more help is coming if this is so (and if needed find more help)
- Discourage the person from moving around or doing anything at all as this may interfere with any physiological discharge, respecting the body's need for being still
- Do not ask any questions about what happened (resist your own tendency to want more information), but remain focused on what is now
- Let the person know that all physical reactions are normal, even good, and will help to release the shock
- Acknowledge any emotions and discourage self-judgement
- Take care of what you need as well!

Bibliography

The Roots of Love: A Guide to Family Constellation by Svagito Liebermeister (Perfect Publisher 2006)

The Zen Way of Counseling: A meditative approach to working with people by Svagito Liebermeister (O-Books 2009)

Osho Therapy: 21 well known therapists describe how their work has been inspired by an enlightened mystic compiled by Svagito (Perfect Publishers 2014)

Re-Awakening of Art: A radical new look at how creativity is born by Meera Hashimoto
(Perfect Publishers 2005)

Dancing into the Unknown: Osho Painting and Art Therapy by Meera Hashimoto
(Perfect Publishers 2017)

Waking the Tiger: Healing Trauma by Peter Levine (North Atlantic Books 1997)

Healing Trauma: A pioneering program for restoring the wisdom of your body by Peter Levine (Sounds True 2008)

In an Unspoken Voice: How the body releases trauma and restores goodness by Peter Levine (North Atlantic Books 2010)

Vigyan Bhairav Tantra Vol I and II: The Book of Secrets, a new commentary by Osho
(The Rebel Publishing House)

Meditation: The First and Last Freedom by Osho (St. Martin's Press, USA)

About the Author

Svagito Liebermeister is a spiritual teacher and psychotherapist who travels every year to more than 15 countries, holding courses and training programmes in Family Constellation, Counselling, Trauma Healing and Male-Female Energywork. He holds a degree in psychology from Munich University, has been teaching for 40 years, and has trained hundreds of practitioners worldwide in the art of working with people.

Since 1980, Svagito has also been a disciple of the Indian Mystic Osho and has been practicing a wide range of meditation techniques, which are the foundation of his work. For many years, he coordinated the Osho Therapist Training Program at the International Osho Meditation Resort in Pune, India, one of the largest personal growth centers in the world.

He was Meera's partner for 25 years and together with her has led numerous courses that combine art, therapy and meditation. After her passing, he founded the Meera Art Foundation (MAF) and the Meera Art Museum (MAM) and together with Meera's assistant team continues Meera's work.

Svagito has published four books that have been translated into 9 languages:

The Roots of Love. A Guide to Family Constellation
The Zen Way of Counseling- a meditative approach to working with people
Osho Therapy- a compilation on therapy and meditation
Dancing into the Unknown by Meera Hashimoto

For further information please visit:

www.family-constellation.net
www.meera-art-foundation.com
https://meera.werkverzeichnis.at

www.ingramcontent.com/pod-product-compliance
Lightning Source LLC
Chambersburg PA
CBHW052211240426
43670CB00036B/121